MILL'S *ON LIBERTY*

Continuum Reader's Guides

MILL'S *ON LIBERTY*
A Reader's Guide

GEOFFREY SCARRE

continuum

Continuum International Publishing Group
The Tower Building   80 Maiden Lane
11 York Road   Suite 704
London SE1 7NX   New York, NY 10038

British Library Cataloguing-in-Publication Data
A catalogue record for this book is available from the British Library.

ISBN: HB: 0–8264–8648–7
9780826486486
PB: 0–8264–8649–5
9780826486493

Library of Congress Cataloguing-in-Publication Data
A catalog record for this book is available from the Library of Congress.

Typeset by YHT Ltd, London
Printed and bound in Great Britain by
MPG Books Ltd, Bodmin, Cornwall

CONTENTS

INTRODUCTORY NOTE

This book is designed to provide a detailed critical reading of *On Liberty* and to explain the reasons for the book's abiding importance to moral and political debate within the liberal tradition. Since its first appearance in 1859, *On Liberty* has been endlessly reprinted and translated into many languages. The standard modern edition of Mill's works is that published in 33 volumes by Toronto University Press; *On Liberty* forms part of volume 18. This edition, however, whilst highly regarded by Mill scholars, is costly to buy, and most readers wanting a copy of *On Liberty* for their personal use are more likely to purchase one of the many excellent inexpensive editions available in bookshops. (A selection of these is listed in Part V of this guide.) Because it would be invidious (as well as inconvenient for those who do not have it) to single out any particular edition as our working text, I have adopted the increasingly common practice of referring to passages in *On Liberty* by chapter and paragraph number alone. On this system, 'III. 4', for instance, refers to chapter III, paragraph 4. This device of citation is a good deal less cumbersome than it might at first appear since Mill, like many Victorian authors, wrote in long paragraphs which are quick and easy to number.

Some sentences from Part I: Context, section i, have been adapted from my biographical note on Mill for the online Literary Encyclopaedia, found at http:www.LitEncy.com. I am grateful to the editor, Dr Robert Clark, for permission to reproduce these.

PART I

CONTEXT

i. JOHN STUART MILL

John Stuart Mill was born in London in 1806 and died there in 1873. He is generally considered to have been the leading British philosopher of the nineteenth century. His powerful defence of empiricist, liberal and utilitarian positions was hugely influential during his lifetime, and set the terms for much of the subsequent debate in these areas. Mill's advocacy of advanced causes (including, most notably, the extension to women of voting rights in parliamentary elections) made him, by his death, a household name even amongst people who had never read his books. Although Mill's reputation suffered a temporary eclipse around the turn of the twentieth century, he currently ranks high among British empiricists (thinkers, that is, who take knowledge to be based solely on experience) for his writings on logic, science and epistemology, while the deep humanity of his ethical and social thought continues to resonate.

Son of the philosopher and historian James Mill, John Stuart was raised in the radical intellectual circle of his father's friend and patron, the utilitarian social reformer Jeremy Bentham. Groomed by James Mill and Bentham to be the standard-bearer of utilitarian values, John Stuart received an extraordinary home education (he began Greek at three and Latin at six) and had published his first articles (on freedom of expression) before his seventeenth birthday. It has been remarked of him that he was a boy who 'never was a boy'. But before Mill was out of his teens, he became deeply disillusioned with what he saw as the soul-destroying narrowness of his elders' views on the good life, which he thought paid too much attention to the rational and calculative aspects of human nature and not enough to the feelings. In 1826, following years of un-relieved hard work as an editorial assistant to Bentham, he suffered a nervous breakdown that marked a critical caesura in his career; as he explains in his posthumously published *Autobiography*, he emerged from this 'mental crisis' thanks in large part to reading the Romantic poets. From that time his thought displayed the strong influence of the Greeks and Romantics as he attempted to graft on to the basic stock of Benthamite welfarism a more adequate con-ception of human possibilities.

Mill wrote prolifically on a wide range of subjects and his works range from substantial treatises down to short newspaper articles and reviews. Books of lasting importance include *A System of Logic* (1843), *Principles of Political Economy* (1848), *On Liberty* (1859), *Considerations on Representative Government* (1861), *Utilitarianism* (1861), *The Subjection of Women* (1869) and *Three Essays on Religion* (1873). Alongside his massive literary output, Mill found time to serve, between 1823 and 1858, in the administrative role of Assistant Examiner in the British East India Company's London headquarters. He was persuaded with difficulty to stand for par-liament in 1865 and sat for three years as the Liberal MP for Westminster. In 1868, after his unsuccessful attempt to incorporate women's suffrage into the 1867 Reform Bill, he lost his seat to the Conservative bookseller W.H. Smith. Mill's only known romantic attachment was to Mrs Harriet Taylor, whom he first met in 1830 and to whom he generously attributed a major influence on his thinking – including, as we shall see, a significant share in the authorship of *On Liberty*. Their relationship probably remained a platonic one until their marriage, following the death of her first husband in 1851. In Harriet, Mill admired 'a complete absence of superstition' and 'strength of noble and elevated feeling', together with 'a highly reverential nature'. Her death from tuberculosis (which she may have caught from Mill) in 1858 at the age of fifty was a blow from which he never fully recovered; he later wrote that her memory was a religion to him and 'her approbation the stan-dard by which, summing up as it does all worthiness, I endeavour to regulate my life'.

Like Bentham and other utilitarians, Mill believed that morally right action was that which tended to increase happiness and diminish misery. In the short treatise *Utilitarianism*, he crisply sums up the 'Greatest Happiness Principle' as holding that actions are right in proportion as they tend to promote happiness, wrong as they tend to produce the reverse of happiness. By happiness is intended pleasure, and the absence of pain; by unhappiness, pain and the privation of pleasure.[1]

However, Mill is careful to stress that pleasures are not all of equal worth, and that the happiest lives involve the deeper satisfactions of 'spiritual perfection' and personal dignity, and the pursuit of beauty, order and truth. For utilitarianism to escape the common charge that its hedonistic account of value showed it to be a 'doctrine worthy only of swine', it was crucial to emphasise that the quality of one's pleasures was much more important than their quantity. Mill sounds almost Aristotelian when he enjoins his readers to satisfy their 'elevated' faculties in preference to their 'animal appetites', and to strive to develop excellence of mind and character – a theme which also figures prominently in *On Liberty*. His subtle analysis of the nature of human happiness served to raise the utilitarian theory of value permanently above the level of simplistic hedonism. Mill argues that happiness is best sought by energetically pursuing worthwhile ends, and that those who look only to gratify their sensual appetites miss out on more valuable satisfactions. Pleasures of 'mere sensation' are far less able to fulfil us than those of 'the intellect, of the feelings and imagination, and of the moral sentiments'.[2]

Mill did not, however, construe utilitarianism's injunction to maximise happiness as sanctioning the making of heavy-handed benevolent interventions into other people's lives. When helping others to live well, we should beware of imposing our own ideas of happiness – however fine – on them. Since a major condition of happiness is that one should be in control of one's own life, it can be misapplied kindness to obtrude our own good offices on others, because it restricts their scope for self-development. Duly respecting other people's individuality requires knowing when to stand back, as well as when to intervene. The significant place that Mill accords to self-development and autonomy in the good life is also apparent in the famous thesis of *On Liberty* that 'the sole end for which mankind are warranted, individually or collectively, in interfering with the liberty of any of their number, is self-protection' (I. 9).

It is striking that Mill's respect for individual liberty did not translate into unqualified support for a universal voting franchise in national or local government elections. Allowing the vote to the very poor or ill-educated, he thought, offered too many hostages to fortune, since men and women in these classes were likely to be politically naive and liable to be swayed by bribery or lying propaganda. Before universal male and female suffrage could be established, people had to be made fit to vote by the elimination of such disadvantages. Although Mill sometimes toyed with the more radical idea of training people to exercise political responsibility by thrusting that responsibility on them, his native caution and fear of political corruption placed limits on his enthusiasm for democracy.

In metaphysics and epistemology, Mill was a lifelong adherent of the 'school of Experience and Association' which denied the existence of a priori knowledge (that is, knowledge derivable by reason alone) and held all knowledge to consist in 'the facts which present themselves to our senses', plus whatever can be legitimately inferred from these. In *A System of Logic*, he attempted to construct an inductive logic sufficiently powerful to make redundant the postulation of an a priori or intuitive basis for any branch of human knowledge. Remarkably, he even sought to show that the laws of deductive logic and mathematics can be known by inductive inference from a sensory basis, though this demonstration is rarely thought nowadays to be cogent.

Mill wrote in a plain, unembellished and jargon-free style that is occasionally ponderous but is, at its best, both pithy and eloquent. (The American philosopher Brand Blanshard commented approvingly that Mill, unlike many thinkers of the last two centuries, wrote 'clearly enough to be found out'.)[3] Mill taught later writers that profound thoughts do not need to be expressed in hard terms and big words, nor passionate sentiments in rant and polemic. The care and lucidity that he brought to the writing of philosophy – in conscious opposition to the obscurity of Kant and his British followers – is another, and far from negligible, part of his abiding contribution to the English-speaking philosophical tradition.

ii. THE BACKGROUND TO *ON LIBERTY*

Mill claimed to have first conceived the idea of writing an essay on liberty while mounting the steps of the ancient Capitol in Rome in January 1855, though it has been suggested that the project may have had an earlier origin in discussions with his wife.[4] In any case, the ultimate genesis of *On Liberty* can be traced much further back in Mill's career, many of its concerns and some of its arguments making their first appearance in writings of his youth and early manhood.

One important stimulus to John Stuart's thinking about liberty and control was the publication in 1820 of his father's influential articles 'Government' and 'Liberty of the Press'. James Mill argued that while government is only legitimate when it seeks to promote the greatest happiness of the greatest number, all governments have a tendency to become tyrannical, since human beings naturally desire that other people should do what *they* want them to do. Hence to prevent despotism by the rulers, checks and balances need to be built into the constitution and free expression of opinion must be allowed to ensure that all sides of every political question will be heard. Other themes from these essays that must have resonated with the young John Stuart were the importance of thinking for oneself and of not accepting other people's ideas just because they were generally approved or fashionable.

The belief in, and love of, individual liberty that John Stuart absorbed from the Benthamite circle coexisted in creative tension with far less libertarian ideas derived from other sources. Mill's version of utilitarianism, as we have seen, is a particularly high-minded kind which seeks to raise the standard of human life to a more exalted mental and moral level. Individuals who are capable of experiencing both 'higher' and 'lower' pleasures, he claims, 'do give a most marked preference to the manner of existence which employs their higher faculties'.[5] The trouble, though, in Mill's view, is that most people are either too ignorant or too indolent to pursue this mode of existence, being content to pursue conventional pleasures and follow the crowd, without worrying about bettering their mind or character. Not only do they lose out on some of the best things that life has to offer, but in an increasingly democratic age, they threaten to establish a 'tyranny of the majority' (a phrase that Mill borrowed from the French writer Alexis de Tocqueville) characterised by a depressing preference for the insipid and mediocre. (Note that for Mill, unlike for most other moralists ancient and modern, the main obstacle to human improvement is not people's craving for sensual pleasure but their taste for the banal, the uninspiring and the 'respectable'). So in an essay on 'Genius' printed in 1832, Mill could lament that the nineteenth century's so-called 'march of intellect' was in reality 'a march towards doing without intellect, and supplying our deficiency of giants by the united efforts of a constantly increasing multitude of dwarfs'.[6]

The question was whether, whatever attractions liberty might have in the abstract, people could safely be allowed to please themselves and live as they wished, or whether they should be guided and governed, for their own and everyone's good, by the more enlightened members of society. John Stuart was familiar with and impressed by a number of contemporary thinkers who argued powerfully for an element of control by the wise of the not-so-wise; these included Coleridge and Carlyle in Britain and Comte and the Saint-Simonians in France. The strength of their impact on him is startlingly apparent in this passage from a letter written in 1831 to his friend John Sterling:

> [I]t is good for man to be ruled: to submit both his body and mind to the guidance of a higher intelligence and virtue ... the direct antithesis of liberalism, which is for making every man his own guide and sovereign master, and letting him think for himself, and do exactly as he judges best for himself.[7]

It may seem hard to credit that such anti-liberal sentiments could emanate from the author of *On Liberty*, a work that celebrates the value of individual self-expression and resists all forms of well-meaning paternalist interference in other people's lives. However, the letter to Sterling represents the furthest point to which Mill travelled along with the apologists for governance by an elite; later, possibly under Harriet's influence, the conviction grew in him that putting great power into any hands, even those of the wisest and best, is a dangerous expedient, being liable to discourage any unorthodox thoughts or novel 'experiments in living'. Yet he retained to the end of his life an uneasiness about the uses that people would make of liberty. For Mill, personal freedom is not an unqualified good but one contingent on its association with good sense and a desire for self-improvement; and the trouble is that not everyone possesses these attributes. John Rees remarks of him that 'there persisted an inner core of conviction that the masses needed guidance ... and were largely incapable of arriving at reasoned opinions'.[8]

One of the main aims of *On Liberty* is thus to reach a stable equilibrium – or as close to one as possible – between the two forces that contended together in Mill's mind: the love of personal liberty and high estimation of the expression of individual nature, and the fear that many, if not most, people are unlikely to make anything very much of themselves or their lives without the help of cleverer heads. This may seem at first as hopeless as trying to square the circle. But Mill believed, and went far to make plausible, the proposition that a certain kind of liberal polity, which provides opportunities and encouragement to people to develop their qualities but does not coerce them into becoming 'better' men and women, affords the best chance of creating a society which is not merely a crowd, and which provides the setting in which some few individuals can become 'giants'. The real measure of the success of *On Liberty* is how well it manages to demonstrate this proposition.

Mill's concern that both state authority and public opinion should be kept in check and prevented from imposing a deadening uniformity on thought and action has been construed by some as indicating a willingness to see some fairly strong measures of control in operation in society, provided that they constrain the vulgar throng rather than the intellectual elite. Thus in a controversial interpretation, Maurice Cowling has suggested that 'Mill was attempting in *On Liberty* to protect the elite from domination by mediocrity'. Because '[c]onvention, custom and the mediocrity of opinion are the enemies in Mill's mythology', the 'freedom' he wishes to see is of a distinctly ambiguous sort, since it is 'given in order to subject men's prejudices to reasoning authority'.[9] Mill, in other words, is only a liberal when it suits him and most of the time is a thinly disguised authoritarian. But this reading is unconvincing. Mill certainly believed and consistently developed the thesis that agents' actions can legitimately be constrained when they cause, or threaten to cause, harm to other people. But he firmly ruled out interfering with people's choices concerning things that affect only themselves; we may sometimes reasonably warn people about the consequences of their acts, or urge them to think again, but that is all. As William Stafford judiciously sums up Mill's position: 'If a man who is committed to improving his fellow citizens is a paternalist, then Mill was one: but he explicitly repudiates *forcing* improvement upon adults.'[10]

It remains to say something about one of the most mysterious aspects of *On Liberty*, the role played in its conception and writing by Mill's wife. The book carries a dedication to Harriet, who is unstintingly credited as 'the inspirer, and in part the author, of all that is best in my writings'. In a section of the *Autobiography* written in 1870, Mill records how, following the 'irreparable loss' of his wife, 'one of my earliest cares was to print and publish the treatise, so much of which was the work of her whom I had lost, and consecrate it to her memory'.[11] He adds: 'I have made no alteration or addition to it, nor shall I ever' (an unusual decision for Mill, who was an inveterate reviser of his works). *On Liberty* clearly had the status of a favourite child:

> The 'Liberty' was more directly and literally our joint production than anything else which bears my name, for there was not a sentence of it which was not several times gone through by us together, turned over in many ways, and carefully weeded of any faults, either in thought or expression, that we detected in it.... With regard to the thoughts, it is difficult to identify any particular part or element as being more hers than all the rest. The whole mode of thinking of which the book was the expression, was emphatically hers. But I also was so thoroughly imbued with it, that the same thoughts naturally occurred to us both. That I was thus penetrated with it, however, I owe in a great degree to her.[12]

In other passages Mill describes his wife's moral and mental qualities in tones of such unqualified adulation that generations of readers have found their credulity taxed. Crediting her with powers that far exceeded his own, he praised her 'perfect mind', her 'vigorous eloquence' and her 'profound knowledge of human nature and discernment and sagacity in practical life'. In spiritual and temperamental characteristics she reminded him of the poet Shelley – though 'in thought and intellect, Shelley, so far as his powers were developed in his short life, was but a child compared with what she ultimately became'.[13] Yet people acquainted with Harriet Mill were unable to find in her the almost preternatural brilliance which her husband ascribed to her, while her extant letters and unpublished essays indicate her to have been a woman of strong and decided views but no outstanding intellectual distinction. Alexander Bain, who knew both of the Mills well, spoke of John Stuart's 'hyperbolical language of unbounded laudation, which has been the cause of so much wonderment'.[14] He also thought that 'there is probably no means of discovering' how far the faults and virtues of the *Liberty* are to be 'partitioned between the two co-operating minds'.[15]

Perhaps the most convincing appraisal of Harriet's contribution to *On Liberty* comes from Gertrude Himmelfarb. She suggests that Bain and others may have confused two issues: Harriet's intellectual ability and her intellectual influence.[16] Allowing that the former was probably not of the highest order, Himmelfarb thinks that Harriet may have been a significant influence on Mill by helping to focus the issues, settle his uncertainties, and generally providing a critical but sympathetic interlocutor with whom he could discuss the matters that engaged him. Although 'the effect of her letters is to cast doubt on her genius and on his judgement', they nevertheless give the impression of 'a sharp mind, personal and intuitive, quick to generalize and pronounce judgement, confident in the correctness of her opinions and not at all diffident in advancing them'.[17] The *Autobiography* records that it was Harriet who weaned Mill away from the 'tendency towards over-government' displayed in his early illiberal phase; and he candidly admits that without her 'I might have become a less thorough radical and democrat than I am'.[18] She assisted him, too, in coming to recognize 'the relative importance of different considerations'.[19] Without Harriet's input, *On Liberty* would undoubtedly have been a very different book – if it had appeared at all. Mill's description of it as a 'joint production' is therefore not so wide of the mark, provided that we understand Harriet as the junior partner in the creative process.

PART II

OVERVIEW OF THEMES

On Liberty is divided into five chapters. Following an introductory chapter in which the 'one very simple principle' of individual liberty is presented, Mill discusses, in order, 'the liberty of thought and discussion', 'individuality, as one of the elements of well-being', 'the limits of the authority of society over the individual', and practical applications of the liberty doctrine. Part III of this book follows Mill's own chapter arrangement.

CHAPTER I: INTRODUCTORY

Mill begins *On Liberty* with a statement of its 'vital question', namely, 'the nature and limits of the power which can be legitimately exercised by society over the individual'. A brief survey of the history of the 'struggle between Liberty and Authority' sets the scene for Mill's characterization of its latest phase, in which the main threat to individual liberty is not the power of kings or nobles but that of the people themselves, organized in a democratic polity. This 'tyranny of the majority' is more insidious than old-style oppression, since it threatens to enslave the soul as well as the body. People mostly think that everyone else should act as they think right, and popular morality enforces, or seeks to enforce, a deadening conformity of conduct. Custom comes to reign supreme and any behaviour that is remotely idiosyncratic or unusual is, at best, disapproved of and, at worst, suppressed.

As a counter to the tendency of public opinion to become more and more oppressive, Mill proposes the principle 'that the sole end for which mankind are warranted, individually or collectively, in interfering with the liberty of action of any of their number, is self-protection'. Not even the individual's own good is a sufficient ground for subjecting him to constraint, unless he is a child (or, Mill adds, more contentiously, a member of a 'backward' society). Where an individual's conduct causes no harm to anyone else, he should be left entirely free to do as he wishes: 'Over himself, over his own body and mind, the individual is sovereign'.

Mill devotes the final pages of the chapter to clarifying and finessing this 'one very simple principle'. Questions arise about the definition of 'harm to others', the limits of prudent intervention to prevent or remove harms, the desirability of compelling people to act in circumstances where *in*action on their part will have unfortunate consequences for others, and the relationship between individual liberty and personal fulfilment. Giving a foretaste of the issues for discussion later in the book, Mill explains that the 'appropriate region of human liberty' has three main domains, namely, freedom of thought and expression, freedom of action, and the (related) freedom to act in concert with other people. All these, he suggests, need to be carefully guarded in an age which is disposed to reward conformity and mediocrity rather than individuality and genius.

CHAPTER II: OF THE LIBERTY OF THOUGHT AND DISCUSSION

Mill argues that no government, however popular, is entitled to prevent the expression of a minority opinion (though it may forbid or punish direct incitements to cause harm to others). To attempt to stamp out an opinion is not only an affront to the liberty of those who hold it but robs mankind as a whole of the opportunity to examine its merits. There are two possibilities to be considered. Either the opinion is true, in which case people are deprived of the opportunity of exchanging error for truth; or it is false, whereupon they lose the chance of gaining a clearer and livelier idea of truth, 'produced by its collision with error'.

Mill proceeds to articulate and defend these twin claims at length. An underlying thesis of the discussion is that truth is most likely to emerge when there is a free market in ideas. Mill roundly criticizes the implicit assumption of infallibility by those who (often with the best of intentions) seek to put down ideas they believe to be incorrect or immoral. Drawing on historical examples, he argues that trying to coerce other people into toeing the orthodox line on religious or moral questions has frequently led to persecution and suffering, loss of genuine insights, and the creation of a stultifying intellectual atmosphere. Even where an opinion is false, its suppression is undesirable since true beliefs appear in sharper relief when they can be contrasted with false ones. People who cannot say why their views are preferable to the alternatives are in no better case than those who believe superstitions. Mill admits that it would be foolish for the layman to dispute with experts about matters requiring technical knowledge. But we should beware of self-styled 'experts' when it comes to such issues as how to live our lives, or what moral standards or religious creed to adopt.

Mill now introduces a third possibility. Often when opinions or theories clash, the truth is not exclusively on one side or the other but divided between them. Where the issues are complex, there is a reasonable presumption that both sides to a dispute have seized on some but not all of the truth. As an illustration, Mill daringly cites the case of Christian ethics, whose 'negative', 'passive' and otherworldly ideals he argues need to be supplemented by some more positive and practical moral principles.

Mill concedes that unlimited freedom of expression is unlikely to put an end to religious or philosophical sectarianism. Yet he thinks that it is better for there to be 'conflict between parts of the truth' than for half of it to be quietly suppressed. Whilst people engaged in argument should treat their opponents with justice and courtesy, the state would be ill-advised to lay down rules for public discussion, since the impartiality of those charged with enforcing them could not be assumed. The 'real morality of public discussion' is thus a matter for the individual conscience rather than a set of rules to be imposed by the state.

CHAPTER III: OF INDIVIDUALITY, AS ONE OF THE ELEMENTS OF WELL-BEING

The third chapter provides an extended argument for 'the absolute and essential importance of human development in its richest diversity'. Individuality, Mill holds, is under threat in a democratic and materialistic age which is unsympathetic to the desire to be different. Custom and convention rule, genius and eccentricity are frowned upon, and 'collective mediocrity' is preferred to the pursuit of the noble and excellent. But these pressures towards conformism should be opposed, for the opportunity to be self-determining is one of the chief ingredients of human happiness.

Human beings are not all cast in the same mould, and it is not appropriate to expect them all to find their good in the same things. People should be allowed the freedom to develop themselves in their own way, since someone who merely falls in with the proposals that others have made for him 'has no character, no more than a steam engine has a character'. Life-plans are, however, subject to the harm principle, and one may not choose a mode of living which causes injury to others. Mill takes issue with the long-standing view (inspired, he suggests, in large part by Calvinistic Christianity) that our spontaneous desires and impulses are basically bad and need to be repressed. Self-will is not an imperfection, and God would not have bestowed human nature on us merely for the purpose of having us subdue it. Whilst liberty should be distinguished from licence, it is absurd to regard the pursuit of personal excellence as a form of self-indulgence.

Individuals also provide the element of originality that every society must have if it is to avoid stagnation. People are needed to 'commence new practices and set the example of more enlightened conduct and better taste and sense in human life'. The problem with static societies such as China or India is precisely that they have discouraged creative innovation. Mill thinks that Victorian Britain is in danger of becoming similarly inhospitable to enterprise and genius (though many of his contemporary readers found his reports of the death of individuality greatly exaggerated).

In the final pages of the chapter, Mill defends in depth a pluralist conception of human well-being, arguing that good lives can take many forms and that the world is a better place for containing a diversity of lifestyles inspired by a variety of ideals. He argues, controversially but plausibly, that in most cases the life that a person has chosen is the best because he or she has chosen it. The standing threat to human advancement is 'the despotism of custom'. Whilst some of Mill's critics have found his attack on custom too uncompromising (for custom can be supportive as well as constraining), his claim that 'the only unfailing and permanent source of improvement is liberty' is argued with impressive force and passion.

CHAPTER IV: OF THE LIMITS TO THE AUTHORITY OF SOCIETY OVER THE INDIVIDUAL

Mill's 'one very simple principle' specifies a single criterion by which restrictions of liberty can be justified. But it is a less simple matter to explain precisely how the principle applies in practice. In Chapter IV Mill endeavours to trace the boundaries of individual liberty in greater detail. 'How much of human life', he asks, 'should be assigned to individuality, and how much to society?' Where does the authority of society begin, and what obligations to society do individuals incur in return for enjoying the benefits it provides?

Mill argues that the state can reasonably insist that citizens render certain services, such as helping to defend the country against external aggression. But he thinks it better in general for people to be encouraged, rather than driven, to contribute to social well-being. He also reiterates his opposition to the paternalistic coercion of people for their own good; while it may frequently be appropriate to admonish or advise people who are letting themselves down, no one is entitled to say to another adult human being that 'he shall not do with his life for his own benefit what he chooses to do with it'. Yet though we must not try to force people to be better – still less punish them for their self-regarding defects – we are entitled to give them a wide berth if we so wish.

Often, however, people's self-regarding faults (e.g. a weakness for drink or gambling) will have further harmful consequences for other people, and then they may merit intervention under the harm principle. But Mill is against punishing individuals merely for incapacitating themselves for doing good or for setting a bad example to others. In the former case, punishment is likely to generate a fruitless resentment, while those who display the painful or degrading effects of their vices provide examples which are usually 'more salutary than hurtful'. Moreover, when society interferes with self-regarding conduct it disapproves of, it tends to do so in the wrong places and behave in a tyrannical, overbearing fashion.

To illustrate and support his general theses about liberty and control, in the second half of the chapter Mill examines a number of specific examples of illegitimate control, actual or attempted. These include the prohibition of pork in Muslim countries, the temperance movement's campaign in Britain and America to ban or limit the sale of alcohol, the attempts by religious bodies to restrict amusements on the Sabbath, and the persecution of members of the Mormon religious sect on account of their unconventional marriage customs. A potential objection to Mill's defence of individual liberty in these pages is that he may be underestimating the role of shared values, practices and institutions in maintaining social cohesiveness. The liberal claim that people should live and let live needs to be weighed against the fact that (in Mill's own words from an earlier work) in all stable political societies there needs to be 'something which men agree in holding sacred'. The degree to which certain common values or standards may be compulsorily enforced, and individual liberty traded away as the price of sustaining social cohesion, is an issue that *On Liberty* may not be wholly successful in resolving.

CHAPTER V: APPLICATIONS

In this chapter, Mill provides 'specimens of illustration' of the main principles defended in the book, plus some additional arguments for them. He also enlarges on his conception of the proper role of government in its dealings with individual citizens. Government is not there to protect us against the setbacks and disappointments that we inevitably suffer in the competitive conditions of a modern capitalist society, but to make sure that competitions are fairly conducted according to rules that ultimately work to the good of all. It should also ensure free trade and the right of individuals to purchase whatever commodities they like (including dangerous drugs), under the standard condition that their use will cause no harm to others.

Mill suggests that 'offences against decency' (e.g. going nude in a public place, to the annoyance of others) may also be prohibited under the harm principle. Whilst it may be questioned whether such 'violations of good manners' are genuine harms, Mill appears to take the view of some contemporary writers that they may be banned because they cause avoidable distress or embarrassment.

He next asks whether those who encourage or enable individuals to perform morally or physically self-harming acts (e.g. the managers of gambling-houses or brothels) should be subject to constraint under the harm principle. In general, he thinks, they should not, because it would be anomalous to punish the accessory to a harmful act but not the principal (e.g. the keeper of the gambling-den but not the gambler).

Mill argues that there should be few, if any, voluntary agreements from which a person might not be allowed to withdraw under certain circumstances. He controversially proposes that this applies even to marriage, though he emphasizes that divorce proceedings should never be undertaken lightly, especially where there are children's interests to be considered. Mill proceeds to discuss parents' responsibilities for their offspring, arguing that the state has the right and duty to constrain them to discharge these properly. Thus a parent who neglects to ensure his child is given a suitable elementary education may be made to do so, or charged with the cost of it. However, the government should not assume the role of educator, since this would be a recipe for state 'despotism over the mind'. In what some may find a startling application of the harm principle, Mill contends that some people may legitimately be forbidden to have children if it appears that any they might have would lead very miserable or degraded lives.

Governments should not aim to be major providers of goods and services to their citizens (beyond protection). It is better for people to supply their own needs, individually or in combination, since this encourages independence and self-reliance. Where state bureaucracies are left to manage affairs, power tends to concentrate at the centre, innovation is stifled, dependency encouraged, and nothing is done quickly or efficiently. Mill proposes that authority should be devolved as far as is practicable to local communities, and that the function of central government should be to advise, to exhort, to inform and to oversee. Such devolved government would allow individuals greater scope to run their own lives, and be more conducive to the development of a richly diverse humanity.

PART III

READING THE TEXT

CHAPTER I: INTRODUCTORY

I. 1–5: A brief history of liberty

Mill opens the first chapter, rather blandly titled 'Introductory', with a crisp statement of the theme of the work. The aim of *On Liberty* is to provide a 'fundamental treatment' of a topic that has been controversial in all ages but which Mill predicts will become 'the vital question of the future', namely, 'Civil or Social Liberty', or 'the nature and limits of the power which can be legitimately exercised by society over the individual' (I. 1). In order to explain the particular form under which the question of liberty presents itself in the mid-nineteenth century, and the reasons for its urgency, Mill commences with an outline history of the 'struggle between Liberty and Authority' from ancient times to the present. Three main periods or phases, he suggests, can be distinguished.

In the earliest period 'the contest was between subjects, or some classes of subjects, and Government', which might be a single ruler or a dominant tribe or caste. While the power of governments was seen as necessary to secure internal security and protection against external enemies, it was also viewed with fear, since governments were more likely to use their power in their own interests rather than in the interests of the governed. As Mill colourfully puts it, while 'the king of the vultures' was accustomed to keep the 'minor harpies' under control, he was no less bent than they were on preying on the flock. In time, two expedients were devised by 'patriots' to alleviate the danger: first, rulers were compelled to recognize certain rights and liberties of their subjects (Mill is probably thinking here of such events as King John's granting of

Magna Carta in 1215); second, constitutional checks were established whereby rulers had to seek the consent of the community or its representatives for their more important acts (I. 2).

he second period saw the growth of the democratic idea that the people should not merely hold rights against their rulers but should appoint their own governors themselves. The institutions of representative government arose when it seemed to men 'much better that the various magistrates of the State should be their tenants or delegates, revocable at their pleasure'. Only in a democratic polity could the people have 'complete security that the powers of government would never be used to their disadvantage'. And since it was not to be expected that people would oppress themselves, there seemed no longer any necessity to limit the power of government: '[t]he nation did not need to be protected against itself. There was no fear of its tyrannising over itself.' Once the principle of self-government was established, the powers of government might safely be allowed to expand, for they would never be used except for the people's good (I. 3). Mill describes this idea as being characteristic of the 'last generation of European liberalism' and as still very popular with many contemporary Continental thinkers.

It is also, Mill considers, profoundly wrong; and the discovery of its falsity is the distinguishing feature of the third period of the struggle between liberty and authority, which has only just commenced. Former liberal thinkers had been so enthralled by the dream of putting power into the hands of the people that they had failed to grasp the vital truth that democratic power, too, could be used oppressively. In Mill's view, enthusiasm for democratic values needs to be tempered with the sober realization that people-power can pose as great a threat to individual liberties as the power of monarchs and nobles. Citing the contemporary United States as a cautionary example ('a democratic republic [occupying] a large portion of the earth's surface'), Mill points out that phrases such as 'self-government' and 'the power of people over themselves' are highly misleading, because 'the "self-government" spoken of is not the government of each by himself, but of each by all the rest'. In a democracy organized on American lines, the 'will of the people' means the will of the majority, or of the most active citizens; and, as Mill says, 'the people, consequently, may desire to oppress a part of their number'. It follows that precautions against the abuse of power are just as necessary in a democratic polity as in communities ruled by kings or oligarchs. 'The limitation ... of the power of government over individuals', thinks Mill, 'loses none of its importance when the holders of power are regularly accountable to the community, that is, to the strongest party therein' (I. 4).

Mill borrows the French historian and sociologist Alexis de Tocqueville's recently coined expression 'the tyranny of the majority' as a striking label for the danger he fears (I. 5). Although Mill only once (in chapter III) refers explicitly to de Tocqueville in *On Liberty*, the influence of the latter's studies of the political systems in America and France is ever present in his own text. The most significant of de Tocqueville's books, his massive *Democracy in America*, the fruit of a lengthy visit to that country, had appeared in two volumes in 1835 and 1840, and Mill had written glowing reviews of each. De Tocqueville's ideas affected Mill profoundly, and he shared the French author's considerable reservations about the benefits of democratic government and of the accompanying development of 'commercial civilization'. A phenomenon that de Tocqueville had observed in America was also, Mill noted, becoming apparent in England, namely 'the growing insignificance of individuals in comparison with the mass'.[1] Whilst older societies had been diverse in nature, the advent of democracy tended to encourage unity and uniformity, hence de Tocqueville and Mill's fear that 'the peculiar characteristics of each individual will be entirely lost in the uniformity of the general aspect'.[2] Mill's view that rule by the majority is no guarantee against political oppression was also clearly prefigured in *Democracy in America*. 'If it be admitted', de Tocqueville had written, 'that a man possessing absolute power may misuse that power by wronging his adversaries, why should not a majority be liable to the same reproach? Men do not change their characters by uniting with one another.' And where the majority have decided that something should be done, then 'however iniquitous or absurd the measure of which you complain, you must submit to it as well as you can'.[3]

Another theme from de Tocqueville also resonated with Mill and is sharply emphasized in *On Liberty*. Like de Tocqueville, Mill was persuaded that the tyranny of the majority is not exercised merely via the overt acts of the 'political functionaries' who represent it (that is, people such as government ministers, MPs, senators, civil servants and other government agents) but even more effectively by the force of public opinion (I. 6). In America, said de Tocqueville, discussion on any question is carried on so long as the majority is undecided; 'but as soon as its decision is irrevocably pronounced, everyone is silent, and the friends as well as the opponents of the measure unite in assenting to its propriety'. Indeed, the tyranny of the majority is actually more oppressive than the old-style forms of tyranny, in which a king might control the body but left the soul of the individual free. 'Such is not the course adopted by tyranny in democratic republics; there the body is left free, and the soul is enslaved.'[4] Mill's own words echo de Tocqueville's very closely:

> Society can and does execute its own mandates: and if it issues wrong mandates instead of right, or any mandates at all in things with which it ought not to meddle, it practises a social tyranny more formidable than many kinds of political oppression, since, though not usually upheld by such extreme penalties, it leaves fewer means of escape, penetrating much more deeply into the details of life, and enslaving the soul itself. (I. 5)

As Alan Ryan has observed, the insidiousness of the tyranny feared by Mill and de Tocqueville arose in part from the fact that 'this was a soft, constant social pressure for conformity rather than a visible political tyranny' that could be fought with conventional weapons.[5] Both men's worry that the human soul is becoming shackled and subservient under democracy stems from a concern with the preservation of private space that is quintessential to modern liberalism. According to another important French writer on liberty, Benjamin Constant de Rebecque, it was precisely the development of this interest that distinguished modern ideas about the proper domain of liberty from ancient ones. In a work entitled *The Spirit of Conquest and Usurpation and Their Relation to European Civilization* (1814), Constant argued that in the Greek and Roman republics, the kind of freedom that men had primarily sought 'consisted in active participation in collective power rather than in the peaceful enjoyment of individual independence'.[6] To be free was, above all, to be a citizen with a share in the business of government. In a small republic such as classical Athens, the ambition to take an active part in government was more easily satisfied than at the present day, when political units are typically far larger and more complex. (Significantly, Constant thought that one of the great mistakes of the French revolutionaries after 1789 was to attempt to replant old-style citizen-government in the much less favourable soil of a vast modern state). But the right to play an active role in republican government came at a price: citizens had to be ready to 'sacrifice their private independence to preserve their political importance and their share in the administration of the state'. For citizen-republics can only prosper when conditions of strict political equality obtain; and to secure these it is essential to 'prevent the increase of fortunes, proscribe distinctions, [and oppose] the influence of wealth, talents and even virtue'.[7]

Constant shrewdly recognized that notions of human flourishing were not fixed but changed with time, and that modern aspirations to freedom were much more sharply focused on liberty within the private sphere than ancient ones had been:

> The ancients found greater satisfactions in their public existence, and fewer in their private life; consequently, when they sacrificed individual to personal liberty, they sacrificed less to gain more. Almost all the pleasures of the moderns lie in their private existence. The immense majority, always excluded from power, necessarily take only a very passing interest in their public existence. Consequently, in imitating the ancients, the moderns would sacrifice more to obtain less.[8]

Although Mill, writing half a century later, did not think that the 'immense majority' either was or should be indifferent to its 'public existence' (and we should bear in mind that Mill, for all his doubts about democracy, supported the extension of the right to vote in parliamentary elections to all educated householders, including, most radically, women), he would entirely have approved of Constant's emphasis on the importance, to modern people, of the private sphere. It was now 'indispensable to a good condition of human affairs' that individual independence should be protected against the undue interference of collective opinion (I. 5). But the hard and pressing problem was to determine the limit of legitimate interference.

I. 6–7: The force of custom

'All that makes existence valuable to any one', says Mill at I. 6, 'depends on the enforcement of restraints upon the actions of other people.' The 'principal question in human affairs' is therefore what rules of conduct should be enforced, either by the operation of law or by the force of public opinion. Important though this question is, it is one on which, in Mill's opinion, scant progress has so far been made. Every age has had something to say about it yet little effort has gone into establishing rational boundaries, since 'the people of any given age and country no more suspect any difficulty in it, than if it were a subject on which mankind had always been agreed'. Although different societies have set the limits of interference in different places, each one takes its own familiar rules to be 'self-evident and self-justifying'. Mill puts this 'universal illusion' down to the 'magical influence of custom', which has the regrettable effect of making thought appear redundant (I. 6).

But how does custom come to be so powerful a force? Mill suggests that a number of factors are responsible. One is that some who, in Mill's slighting description, 'aspire to the character of philosophers' (and so who ought to know better) have 'encouraged people to believe that 'their feelings, on subjects of this nature, are better than reasons, and render reasons unnecessary'. And where people find they have similar feelings, these readily become the standard of conduct to which everyone is expected to conform. Hence:

> The practical principle which guides them to their opinions on the regulation of human conduct, is the feeling in each person's mind that everybody should be required to act as he, and those with whom he sympathizes, would like them to act (I. 6).

It is this principle, as we shall shortly see, which Mill wishes to replace with a more rational alternative.

Mill pauses briefly to consider the origins of people's views about conduct. Rather few of these, he thinks, have much basis in reason. The common grounds of opinions include prejudices and superstitions, social and antisocial affections, envy and jealousy, arrogance and contemptuousness, and – most importantly – self-interest. 'Among so many baser influences', Mill claims, 'the general and obvious interests of society have of course had a share, and a large one, in the direction of the moral sentiments'. Where one class is socially dominant, its interests play a particularly significant role in shaping the popular morality, and one that is typically assisted by 'the servility of mankind towards the supposed preferences of their temporal masters or of their gods' (I. 6).

Mill's pessimistic assessment of the deadening effect on thought of the power of custom raised eyebrows amongst his Victorian readers. Several of the early reviewers of *On Liberty* accused him of overstating the danger of a socially imposed conformity of opinion in what they perceived as the intellectually lively conditions of mid-nineteenth-century Britain. For instance, Richard Holt Hutton, writing in *The National Review* shortly after *On Liberty*'s publica tion, after noting Mill's fear of 'an increasing despotism of social and political masses over the moral and intellectual freedom of individuals', called this depressing conclusion 'singularly hasty, and utterly unsustained by the premises he lays down'.[9] Another reviewer, Richard William Church, concurred in finding Mill's negative view of custom exaggerated. 'Custom is very powerful', wrote Church in *Bentley's Quarterly Review* in 1860, 'but not omnipotent. The current which runs through society is neither so uniform nor so irresistible as he makes it.'[10]

Mill appears to have taken these criticisms seriously, though he professed to find them ultimately unpersuasive. In a portion of his *Autobiography* written around 1870, he explains that the worries voiced in *On Liberty* were focused more on the probable future rather than the present state of things:

> The fears we expressed, lest the inevitable growth of social equality and of the government of social opinion, should impose on mankind an oppressive yoke of uniformity in opinion and practice, might easily have appeared chimerical to those who looked more at present facts than at tendencies; for the gradual revolution that is taking place in society and institutions has, thus far, been decidedly favourable to the development of new opinions, and has procured for them a much more unprejudiced hearing than they previously met with. But this is a feature belonging to periods of transition, when old notions and feelings have been unsettled, and no new doctrines have yet succeeded to their ascendancy.[11]

This attempt at clarification is not entirely satisfactory. The suggestion that, though a social tyranny of thought has not yet arisen, it surely will, unless prevented, may sound like special pleading. One may also be forgiven for wondering how Mill can be so sure that a period of relative stasis is just around the corner, when 'some particular body of doctrine rallies the majority around it, organizes social institutions and modes of action conformably to itself', and adds reinforcement by throwing the whole weight of public education behind it.[12] But even if, like Mill's contemporary readers, we doubt whether his fears for the future were wholly supported by the evidence available to him, we need not question the sincerity of those fears. Realistically or not, Mill believed that habits of free thought were not yet sufficiently well-established to be secure against the advocates of new orthodoxies.

Mill admits one partial but important exception to his general condemnation of the dead hand of custom on moral opinion. In the single area of religious belief and practice, some progress has been made towards establishing a principle of freedom of thought and conscience, and centuries of conflict have finally issued in an agreement to differ. 'It is accordingly on this battle field, almost solely', says Mill, 'that the rights of the individual against society have been asserted on broad grounds of principle, and the claims of society to exercise authority over dissentients openly controverted'. Even so, the growth of religious toleration also owes something to the increasing public indifference towards religion – 'so natural in mankind is intolerance in whatever they really care about'. 'Wherever the sentiment of the majority is still genuine and intense', he contends, 'it is found to have abated little of its claim to be obeyed.' Moreover, those who do show toleration often do so 'with tacit reserves': for example, some Protestants are willing to tolerate most other kinds of Protestant but stop short at toleration of Roman Catholics or Unitarians (I. 7).

A century and a half before *On Liberty*, the philosopher John Locke had argued that 'It is only light and evidence that can work change in men's opinions; which light can in no manner proceed from corporal sufferings, or any other outward penalties.'[13] Mill would have applauded the sentiment, but doubted the extent to which, by the 1850s, it had been popularly absorbed, even in a relatively liberal country such as Britain. People might no longer be burned at the stake for holding dissentient religious opinions but petty and bad-tempered intolerance remained a widespread phenomenon in Mill's day. One not untypical case is reported by *The Illustrated London News* in the very year in which *On Liberty* appeared. When a Rector of markedly high-church leanings attempted to hold Sunday services at the newly consecrated, and distinctly low-church (i.e. evangelical), St Matthew's in Pell Street, London, a remarkable rumpus ensued. When the Rector, accompanied by a troup of choristers, bowed to the altar and said the words 'In the name of the Father, the Son, and the Holy Ghost' instead of the usual prayers, he was greeted by 'hisses, stamping of feet, and the slamming of pew doors'. When, at another service later that same day, the Rector again appeared with his choristers in the church,

> a loud, determined shout of disapproval burst forth. Unmoved, however, by this violent demonstration, the rev. gentleman knelt before the altar and went through the Litany service. He was hissed, hooted, and yelled at during the whole of the service, and at its close made his way with difficulty to the vestry.[14]

Only when the Rector thought better of trying to conduct the evening service that same day did a large crowd that had assembled to barrack him (or worse) quietly disperse. Intolerance was clearly alive and thriving in the London of 1859.

I. 8–10: 'One very simple principle'

'In England', suggests Mill, 'from the peculiar circumstances of our political history, though the yoke of opinion is perhaps heavier, that of law is lighter, than in most other countries of Europe' (I. 8). Mill presumably has in mind the constitutional settlement reached in 1689, in the so-called Glorious Revolution, that finally put English liberties on a firm legal footing following the flight of King James II. Since the end of the seventeenth century, Englishmen had been keenly jealous of their rights and unwilling to allow the legislative or executive arms of government to interfere with individual liberty beyond the most minimal extent. (English *women*, on the other hand, were subjected to far greater legal restrictions and were still expected, in the mid-Victorian period, to be subservient to the will of their fathers or husbands). Mill notes with some regret that the basis of Englishmen's attitudes is not any principled regard for the independence of the individual but instead 'the still subsisting habit of looking on government as representing an opposite interest to the public'. When the majority start to think of the government as *their* government, this habit can be expected to change and the tentacles of government be allowed to extend much further into the private sphere. (If Mill's projection is right, this phase of diminishing freedom will form the *fourth* stage in the history of the struggle between liberty and authority). In Mill's view it is vital, before this happens, to clarify the limits of legitimate government intervention. Striking a note that can easily be overlooked by hasty readers of *On Liberty*, he considers that there are cases where government *ought* to interfere where customarily it does not. Since government should serve the public good, there are areas of life in which the agencies of the state ought to be *more* rather than less interventionist than they are. These words of Mill provide a salutary reminder that it is wrong to look on him, as some people do, as an early exponent of the idea of 'hands-off' government favoured by many modern libertarians. As we shall see, he is prepared to countenance a much more capacious role for government than libertarian thinkers of our own time would like. Mill is opposed not to government as such but to the abusive expansion of its powers into domains which are not its rightful concern.

But what are the areas into which neither government nor the coercive force of public opinion should intrude? Where, in other words, should the bounds of individual liberty be set? Mill's answer is contained in a justly celebrated passage:

> The object of this Essay is to assert one very simple principle, as entitled to govern absolutely the dealings of society with the individual in the way of compulsion and control, whether the means used be physical force in the form of legal penalties, or the moral coercion of public opinion. That principle is, that the sole end for which mankind are warranted, individually or collectively, in interfering with the liberty of action of any of their number, is self-protection. That the only purpose for which power can be rightfully exercised over any member of a civilized community, against his will, is to prevent harm to others. His own good, either physical or moral, is not a sufficient warrant. He cannot rightfully be compelled to do or forbear because it will be better for him to do so, because it will make him happier, because, in the opinions of others, to do so would be wise, or even right ... The only part of the conduct of any one, for which he is amenable to society, is that which concerns himself. In the part which merely concerns himself, his independence is, of right, absolute. Over himself, over his own body and mind, the individual is sovereign. (I. 9)

These famous words have been endlessly discussed and debated. The principle at their heart – which is often referred to as Mill's 'harm principle' – at first sight merits their author's description of it as 'very simple'. What could be more straightforward than the claim that people may never be coerced in their own interests, but only to prevent their harming others? And what could seem initially more attractive than the idea that we should be allowed to get on with our lives as we wish, provided that in pursuing our own goals we do no harm to anyone else? Yet, as generations of commentators have pointed out, Mill's principle is neither so easy to interpret nor so morally unproblematic as it may at first appear.

What exactly, for instance, does Mill understand by his use of the word 'harm'? Many philosophers favour a rather broad characterization of the idea of harm in terms of a setback to interests. But should we hold that just *any* setback to an interest is a harm against which we ought, where practicable, to be protected? It is fairly uncontroversial that physical violence, rape, kidnapping, theft and swindling are kinds of harm which, under the principle, may legitimately be prevented or discouraged by appropriate agents or agencies (e.g. the law or the police force). But am I 'harmed' if I am confronted with indecent behaviour in the street, or if others speak insultingly about the objects of my religious convictions? (I do, after all, have an *interest* in not being exposed to disgusting behaviour or in hearing my religion treated with disrespect). Should the state treat as harmful and seek to ban the publication of material that offends members of a particular religion, race, gender, or other social grouping? (Does it make a difference whether the offence that such material would cause is intentional or inadvertent?) Or should acts and practices that 'merely' offend not be counted as harms (though they set back interests) even in an extended sense, and consequently be excluded from the scope of the harm principle? This is an issue we shall have to return to later in this book.

Does the category of harms that may legitimately be prevented also extend to what would normally be termed 'nuisances', such as playing loud music in public on one's ghetto-blaster, taking calls on one's cell-phone in the middle of a play or concert, or allowing the trees in one's garden to grow so large that they badly restrict a neighbour's light? There is no principled reason why it should not, though people cannot reasonably expect to be protected against just *anything* that they happen to find annoying. For instance, if, owing to my fastidious colour sense, I am pained by seeing people dressed in bright red clothes, I am not entitled to demand that the police prevent the wearing of scarlet socks or vermilion sweaters in the places I frequent. Here the problem lies with me rather than with the people whose dress I object to, and I need to become both more tolerant and more aesthetically broad-minded. Sometimes, for the sake of peaceful community relations, it is better for us to grin and bear what we consider nuisances rather than seek to have them forbidden. But this is not always so, and since a minor harm is still a harm, it need not be an unwarranted interference with individual liberty to prevent people causing a nuisance to others.

Again, when do forms of commercial exploitation that are typical of capitalist societies count as 'harms' calling for state intervention? Am I harmed if the aggressive practices of a major supermarket chain have caused the closure of all the small grocery shops in my district, leaving me with no practicable alternative but to shop at their store? It may be more evident that the owners of the shops that have been forced out of business have been harmed by their giant rival's activities. But should the government of a capitalist country impose tight restraints on commercial behaviour in order to prevent such harms as these? If it were to, then it would arguably do more harm than good, by endangering the benefits that free markets are capable of providing. At this juncture it is worth noticing that Mill does not assert that harms to others *must*, wherever possible, be prevented, but only that they *may* be – that is, the harm principle lays down a necessary condition for preventive intervention rather than a sufficient one. This is an important point, and it works both in Mill's favour and against it. Since Mill does not say that competent agents and agencies are *always* obliged to halt harmful behaviour when they can, he leaves it open that it is better to allow some harms to occur, because of the excessive cost to individuals or society as a whole of preventing them. This helps to make Mill's position on liberty more thoroughly consistent with his general utilitarian approach to issues of social welfare. However, if the harm principle states only a necessary and not also a sufficient condition for intervention in the affairs of others, then it does not supply all that Mill was looking for when he spoke of the need for a principle that would clearly delineate the boundary between proper and improper curtailments of liberty.

Problematic for a different reason is a limitation that Mill proceeds, in the very next paragraph, to impose on the scope of his 'very simple' principle. 'It is, perhaps, hardly necessary to say', he writes, 'that this doctrine is meant to apply only to human beings in the maturity of their faculties.' It does not apply to children or to 'young persons below the age which the law may fix as that of manhood or womanhood' (I. 10). Nor – more surprisingly, we may think – does it apply in the case of 'those backward states of society, in which the race itself may be considered as in its nonage' (i.e. its youth – the opposite of dotage). But an even more startling sentence shortly follows: 'Despotism', Mill says, 'is a legitimate mode of government in dealing with barbarians, provided the end be their improvement, and the means justified by actually effecting that end.' In fact, the principle of liberty has 'no application' before 'mankind have become capable of being improved by free and equal discussion.' Until a people arrive at that happy state, 'there is nothing for them but implicit obedience to an Akbar or a Charlemagne [for Mill, examples of enlightened rulers], if they are so fortunate as to find one' (I. 10). In the world of the nineteenth century, Mill expects the benevolent, despotic rule over 'backward' peoples to be exercised by advanced nations such as Britain.

Mill's view that children's liberty should be restricted in their own interests (a position known as 'paternalism', from the Latin word *pater*, meaning 'father') has generally gone down better with his readers than his parallel proposal with regard to 'barbarians' and people living in 'backward states of society'. Children, especially when very young, lack the knowledge and mental competence to be safely allowed to be self-determining; as Mill observes, they need to be taken care of by others, and to be 'protected against their own actions as well as against external injury'. If children were placed under no restraints and allowed to do anything they wanted, probably few of them would survive to maturity. Common sense dictates that if they are ever to become autonomous, or self-determining, adults, their liberty must be limited during their immature years. Joel Feinberg speaks of a child's right to autonomy (his right to make decisions for himself) as a right that is, in effect, being held in trust for him until he is of an age to exercise it wisely.[15] Mill is not, therefore, asserting that, in the case of children, safety and security count for more than autonomy whereas in that of adults they count for less. His position is the more consistent one that restricting children's liberty while developing their abilities and educating them in the ways of the world maximizes their potential for autonomous individuality at a later date.

It is much less clear, however, that such an argument can justify Mill's paternalist stance with regard to adult people living in pre-modern (Mill's 'backward') societies. In 1859 the British Empire was large and still growing; it already included major parts of Africa and Asia (including India), North America, Australia and New Zealand. Mill believed the British imperium to be, on the whole, a good thing, that brought, or promised to bring, the benefits of advanced western civilization to places where life was, for the majority of people, blighted by the evils of poverty, oppression, ignorance and disease. (Things could occasionally go wrong even in the best-regulated empires, and Mill was at the forefront of protest in 1865 when Governor Eyre of Jamaica put down with great brutality an insurrection by the island's grossly exploited plantation workers). Nowadays we are likely to find Mill's cool assumption that 'Britain knows best' and his contemptuously dismissive attitude to non-European values and ways of living naive as well as patronising; yet his vision of empire, unlike some, had the saving grace of being fundamentally benevolent. But, whatever Mill thought, adult Indians or Africans are not children, and it would not follow that they should be treated as such *even if* their societies were, as Mill held, in some meaningful sense immature (a claim hard to sustain in the case of such sophisticated and ancient cultures as those of India and China). Nor could it be said that the rights to autonomy of individuals were, like those of children, being held in trust for them until they attained a state of cultural adulthood; for Mill thought that this was a process that would take several generations.

As some of Mill's contemporary critics pointed out, it is very implausible to suppose that *all* adult Britons are capable of making mature and sensible choices (and should therefore be allowed to do so) while *no* adult Indians or Africans are. In James Fitzjames Stephen's view, if a paternalistic 'principle of compulsion' was justified, as Mill claimed, in regard to children and 'backward' races, it was 'impossible' not to extend it to the case of foolish or unwise adults back home. 'Mr Mill', said Stephen, 'ought to have proved that there are among us no considerable differences in point of wisdom'; yet everyone knows that '[o]ne person may be more mature at fifteen than another at thirty'. In any case, why should

Mill believe that Indians or Africans were not capable of taking part in 'free and equal discussion' (whatever exactly he envisaged under that label)? 'The wildest savages, the most immature youths, capable of any sort of education', thought Stephen, 'are capable of being improved by free discussion upon a great variety of subjects.' Mill's position was therefore strained and inconsistent, and Stephen reasonably wondered what there was 'in the character of a very commonplace ignorant peasant or petty shopkeeper in these days which makes him a less fit subject for coercion on Mr Mill's principle than the Hindoo nobles and princes who were coerced by Akbar?'[16] Either both should be held subject to paternalistic coercion, or neither should be.

How original was Mill's 'one very simple principle'? Not at all, in Mill's own opinion. The importance of *On Liberty* lay not in its saying something that had never been said before, but in its emphatically repeating the message at a time of social transformation. 'The leading thought of the book', he reflected in his *Autobiography*, 'is one which though in many ages confined to insulated thinkers, mankind have probably at no time since the beginning of civilization been entirely without.'[17] Rarely, if ever, though, had it been more crucial to defend the doctrine of individual liberty than in Victoria's realm, where the tyranny of the majority threatened to impose 'an oppressive yoke of uniformity in opinion and practice'.

Possibly the closest precedent for the harm principle, at least amongst British writers, is to be found in Locke's *Letter Concerning Toleration*, published in Latin in 1689 and in English the following year. Although Locke was concerned with the specific topic of religious toleration, the principle of non-interference he propounded anticipates Mill's broader principle in structure and substance. Noting that one man's religious beliefs and mode of worship have no bearing on whether others will be saved, Locke declared that 'the care of each man's salvation belongs only to himself'. Other people, if they think him to be mistaken, may, and should, charitably admonish him and affectionately attempt to recall him from his errors. But –

all force and compulsion are to be foreborne. Nothing is to be done imperiously. Nobody is obliged in that matter to yield obedience unto the admonitions or injunctions of another, further than he himself is persuaded. Every man in that has the supreme and absolute authority of judging for himself. And the reason is because nobody else is concerned in it, nor can receive any prejudice from his conduct therein.[18]

Locke's powerful (and at the time radical) statement that we are each responsible for our own salvation and not for anyone else's is enlarged by Mill into the proposition that we are individually responsible for the direction of all aspects of our own lives. Both writers locate the only limiting condition on our freedom to choose for ourselves in the duty to refrain from doing any harm to others. And both display their firm allegiance to the ideal of individual autonomy that is central to the liberal tradition. Mill describes *On Liberty* in the *Autobiography* as 'a kind of philosophic text-book of a single truth' of vital significance in changing times, namely 'the importance, to man and society, of a large variety of kinds of character, and of giving full freedom to human nature to expand itself in innumerable and conflicting directions'.[19] Only if people were allowed to make choices for themselves would they develop as individuals, and the main purpose of government was to promote autonomy by ensuring that it could be maximally exercised. Mill would have approved of the reading of the harm principle offered by the present-day political philosopher Joseph Raz, who sees the state's role as that of securing the conditions of autonomous action. 'Using coercion', writes Raz, 'invades autonomy and thus defeats the purpose of promoting it, *unless it is done to promote autonomy by preventing harm.*'[20]

I. 11–16: Freedom and constraint in modern society
Mill devotes the final paragraphs of his first chapter to providing some more detailed comment on the areas in which, in modern society, people ought to be allowed to follow their own preferences, and those in which they may legitimately be subjected to external control. But first he inserts an important clarification. Whilst talking about *rights* to liberty is quite acceptable, it is wrong, Mill contends, to conceive of rights as possessing some form of existence 'independent of utility' (I. 11). Like Jeremy Bentham before him, Mill regarded the idea that there existed abstract rights as a metaphysical mistake (Bentham famously dismissed talk of such rights as 'rhetorical nonsense – nonsense on stilts').[21] In Mill's view, the notion of rights is properly subordinate to that of utility – that is,

roughly, public well-being or happiness – and rights claims should always be adjudicated by reference to the utilitarian standard of how well they promote the general welfare. (To give a rather obvious example of how this works, if someone were to claim that he had a right to take whatever goods he wanted out of other people's houses, Bentham and Mill would respond that he does not possess such a right, since such behaviour would undermine the socially useful institution of private property as well as distressing those who lose their goods).

An issue which has been much discussed in relation to *On Liberty* is whether Mill's stalwart defence of individual freedom is quite consistent with his utilitarianism. On a superficial view, it seems that there can be occasions on which the demands of liberty and of utility pull in different directions. For instance, some paternalistic interventions to prevent people harming themselves by over-indulgence in drink or drugs may appear justified on utilitarian grounds though they are not admissible according to the harm principle (unless, of course, the drinker or drug-taker's habit leads him or her to cause injury to other people). It may also seem that utilitarians should favour the coercion of lazy or careless people who are capable of making a substantial contribution to the public good to cast off their indolent ways and start doing their bit. But, as Mill explains, these appearances of conflict between liberty and utility disappear once we take a more probing view.

Utility, Mill emphasizes, is 'the ultimate appeal on ethical questions' – 'but it must be utility in the largest sense, grounded on the permanent interests of man as a progressive being' (I. 11). This impressive-sounding, if rather vague, formulation is quickly clarified. A human being will not advance in qualities of mind or character through being coerced to improve himself. Real improvement is self-improvement, and cannot be enforced. More-over, the most effective agents of good are not those who are compelled to exert themselves in the public interest; encouraging and persuading people to promote utility is generally more pro-ductive than trying to twist their arms (which also generates resentment). In thinking about the maximization of utility, we need to consider what kind of world we wish to live in. For Mill, a happy and flourishing society is one which has attained a certain threshold of cultural sophistication and whose members are spontaneous, self-directing individuals, as fully in control of their own lives as is consistent with their respecting the similar autonomy of others. Occasionally they will make choices which are sub-optimal or even positively damaging to themselves; but most people still prefer to be allowed to make their own mistakes rather than be subjected to the demeaning, if well-meant, paternalist control of others. As John Gray explains, in Mill, 'liberal principles are adopted as rational strategies for the maximal promotion of well-being – as devices for the maximization of utility'.[22]

Mill concedes, however, that there are some kinds of acts that people may, at least in principle, rightly be compelled to perform, on the ground that *inaction* on their part would, or could, be injurious to others. These include giving evidence in a court of law, sharing in the common defence or in 'any other joint work necessary to the interest of the society' whose protection they enjoy, saving a fellow-creature's life, or interposing to defend the weak against ill-usage (I. 11). But Mill is characteristically wary of maintaining that people should *in practice* be coerced into preventing evil, since it is always possible that 'the attempt to exercise control would produce other evils, greater than those which it would prevent'. 'To make any one answerable for doing evil to others is the rule', he remarks; 'to make him answerable for not preventing evil is, comparatively speaking, the exception'. Mill leaves it finally unclear whether he thinks that it would, all things considered, be reasonable to compel people to come to the aid of those in danger or distress (and perhaps to punish them if they fail to do so). Probably he believes that particular cases should be decided on their own merits. But he does not doubt that if no compulsion is exerted, 'the conscience of the agent himself should step into the vacant judgement seat' (I. 11). Good moral agents will act well without having to be made to.

Mill is also adamant that society should refrain altogether from interference 'in all that portion of a person's life and conduct which affects only himself, or if it also affects others, only with their free, voluntary, and undeceived consent and participation'. He admits, however, that whatever affects one person may affect other people through him, and that such 'indirect' effects can complicate the moral issues; but these difficulties he postpones for further discussion 'in the sequel' (i.e. chapter IV).

Mill proposes dividing what he calls the 'appropriate region of human liberty' into three chief domains. First is 'the inward domain of consciousness', which comprehends freedom of conscience, freedom to think and feel what we want, liberty to form our own views 'on all subjects, practical or speculative, scientific, moral, or theological'; and also, as an associated freedom, the liberty to express and publish our own opinions to the world. The second domain concerns liberty of individual action and includes the freedoms to frame our own plan of life, to follow our own tastes and pursuits, and in general to do what we like, so long as our acts and choices cause no harm to other people. This second domain is also the basis of the third, since what people are free to do individually, they must also be free to do conjointly. There should therefore be 'freedom to unite, for any purpose not involving harm to others: the persons combining being supposed to be of full age, and not forced or deceived' (I. 12).

These areas of freedom need to be sedulously maintained and protected in an age in which, on Mill's reading of the signs, society is becoming more rather than less oppressive of the individual, forcing him to act only in the ways it approves and imposing on him its own 'notions of personal as well as of social excellence' (I. 12). For:

> [t]he only freedom which deserves the name, is that of pursuing our own good in our own way, so long as we do not attempt to deprive others of theirs, or impede their efforts to obtain it. Each is the proper guardian of his own health, whether bodily, *or* mental and spiritual. (I. 13)

Mill is acutely aware that the attacks on liberty he fears are backed in large part by benevolent intentions. This is what makes them so dangerous. Those who wish to trammel individual freedom (and they include not just supporters of religion but also the prophets of new forms of social organization such as the French philosopher Auguste Comte) justify the restrictions they favour on the grounds that they are in people's best interests, and so what they ought to desire for themselves. This appeal to the individual's good makes their assault on freedom even more insidious, since it helps to obscure the real damage it does to individuality.

Mill's passionate advocacy of the value of individualism might well be questioned, as indeed it was by some of his earliest critics. Even Mill's more sympathetic commentators have sometimes worried that he draws no adequate distinction between individuality and mere eccentricity. Not all distinctive personalities and ways of life appear particularly valuable, to an unprejudiced eye. And while it is doubtless good for us to pursue our own good in our own way, not everyone, if left to themselves, will pursue anything that is very recognizable as good. 'As if it were a sin to control, or coerce into better methods, human swine in any way; . . . *Ach, Gott in Himmel!*' exclaimed Thomas Carlyle on first reading *On Liberty*; and while we may object to Carlyle's description of human beings as swine, we may share his concern that people are not always particularly adept at identifying their own best interests.[23]

Mill, however, leaves further discussion of the merits of individualism, and of the problems associated with it, to his third chapter. In the meanwhile, chapter II will be devoted to the subject of 'Liberty of Thought, from which it is impossible to separate the cognate liberty of speaking and writing'. This, as Mill admits, is a familiar stamping-ground for proponents of liberty; but the importance of the topic, he trusts, will be thought to justify his venturing 'on one discussion more' (I. 16).

Study Questions

1. Is it ever justifiable to coerce people in their own interests?
2. Should people ever be compelled to help others?
3. Does Mill convincingly defend the thesis of 'the tyranny of the majority'?
4. Can an adequate utilitarian justification be given of Mill's 'harm principle'?

CHAPTER II: OF THE LIBERTY OF THOUGHT AND DISCUSSION

II. 1–2: The rejection of censorship

Chapter II of *On Liberty* is by far the longest in the book and could almost stand as a treatise in its own right, independent of the parent work. Mill's robust and spirited defence of the free expression of opinion is perhaps the most significant contribution to its subject ever made, and retains to this day its capacity both to inspire and provoke. Yet, for all the clarity and brilliance of its argumentation, chapter II presents the reader of *On Liberty* with some puzzles. It is not always entirely easy to see how the ideas and concerns of the second chapter relate to those of the book as a whole; connections are left implicit which might more helpfully have been made explicit; moreover, the fairly uncompromising nature of Mill's defence of free speech may be in some tension, as various critics have pointed out, with a strict maintenance of the harm principle from chapter I (for speech can sometime stimulate actions that lead to the harming of others). We shall pick up on these points as we proceed.

Mill begins with an upbeat report on progress in the long-running struggle for the freedom of the press to discuss political affairs. Although repressive laws remain on the statute book, they are rarely invoked any more except 'when fear of insurrection during some temporary panic drives ministers and judges from their propriety'. But while this is a development to be welcomed, a new danger looms. In the present age of liberty (the third, according to the chronology outlined in chapter I), the chief worry is that a government which speaks for the people will use its power to enforce the views that are popular with the public and seek to stifle the expression of any dissenting views. It would be a further instance of the growing tyranny of the majority if minority or unpopular opinions were to be routinely suppressed. Such a use of power by government on behalf of the people, Mill contends, must always be noxious and illegitimate. As a counter to such a tendency, he affirms a noble general principle:

> If all mankind minus one were of one opinion, mankind would be no more justified in silencing that one person than he, if he had the power, would be justified in silencing mankind. (II. 1)

Suppressing minority opinions is not only an affront to the liberty of those who hold them: it is also wrong for the more utilitarian reason that 'it is robbing the human race, posterity as well as the existing generation – those who dissent from the opinion, still more than those who hold it'. Either the suppressed opinion is true or it is false (we should note here that later in the chapter, at paragraph 34, Mill adds a third possibility, that it may be a mixture of both). If it is true, then people lose the opportunity of substituting truth for error. If it is false, then they forfeit 'what is almost as great a benefit', namely the opportunity of gaining a 'clearer perception and livelier impression of truth produced by its collision with error'.

These might be described as 'epistemic' benefits arising from the free expression and exchange of ideas (from Greek *episteme*, meaning belief), since they serve in the acquisition of true beliefs and the avoidance of falsehoods. But it is striking that Mill says nothing about a further reason why freedom of expression might be considered a significant good, namely that speakers manifest their individuality when they exercise it. In view of the importance that Mill accords to individuality elsewhere in *On Liberty*, his silence at this point is unexpected. If people are not permitted to speak their own minds but are compelled to toe the approved line or remain silent, then they are not being treated with the respect due to individuals capable of autonomous judgement and action. Moreover, if what they (wish to) say causes no harm to others, then such suppression or censorship is also in flagrant contravention of the harm principle – yet Mill oddly omits to point this out. John Gray has suggested that Mill 'regards freedom of expression as partly constitutive of autonomous agency', but, if he does, he leaves his view to be inferred from other chapters of *On Liberty* (and particularly chapter III, 'Of individuality'), since chapter II – where one would look to find it defended – is strangely reticent on the subject.[1]

In a footnote to II. 1, Mill refers to the Government Press Prosecutions of 1858 which followed publication of an article defending the allegedly immoral doctrine that it is lawful to kill a tyrannical ruler. Although the prosecutions were dropped, Mill thinks that they should never have been brought. Describing the legitimacy of tyrannicide as 'at all times one of the open questions of morals' (and so a fit subject for discussion), Mill adds that 'the instigation to it, in a specific case' may be worthy of punishment, but only where it can be shown to have given rise to 'an overt act' (i.e. an actual attempt at assassination). On the basis of this passage we might think that Mill believes that no speech or writing, no matter how inflammatory, merits punishment or even restriction *unless and until* it succeeds in inciting some violent or otherwise harmful act. Yet at the opening of chapter III Mill takes a less libertarian view, proposing that 'opinions lose their immunity [i.e. to suppression or prosecution] when the circumstances in which they are expressed are such as to constitute their expression a positive instigation to some mischievous act' (III. 1). Opinions, in other words, may be suppressed or punished when they are merely *liable* to cause mischievous behaviour. Mill contends that there is a big difference between arguing in the press that corn dealers are starvers of the poor, and delivering the same message orally or in the form of a placard 'to an excited mob assembled before the house of a corn dealer'. People must not abuse their liberty by making themselves a nuisance to others, and those who do so may need to be controlled by 'the unfavourable sentiments' or even 'the active interference of mankind' (III. 1).

Presumably Mill would also regard it as unacceptable instigation to mischief to urge in a series of inflammatory newspaper articles that greedy corn dealers should all be hanged from the nearest lamp-post. Incitement to offend need not necessarily occur on the spot. But this raises the question – which Mill scarcely addresses – of where legitimate free expression ends. Would it be acceptable if the newspaper writer said only that corn dealers deserved to feel the public's wrath? Or might this turn upon where he said it and to whom – whether he voiced the opinion in the sedate columns of *The Times* or in a populist rag read by people already known to be violently incensed against the corn dealers? Since any condemnatory statement is liable to stimulate negative feelings towards its target, the problem is to establish reasonable limits to expression that provide requisite protections in line with the harm principle yet do not constrict free expression to more than the most minimal degree necessary for attaining that aim. As a number of commentators have noted, Mill is less forthcoming than he might be here. C.L. Ten remarks that '[Mill's] liberal theory is incomplete unless it is supplemented with a more detailed examination of the types of restrictions which it would allow'.[2] And Gray complains that '[w]hat Mill lacks ... are criteria to distinguish incitement to act from advocacy and debate about the merits of action'.[3]

One might think that a straightforward application of the harm principle would be all that was needed to determine the proper limits to free speech. But we should remember that Mill considers the principle to supply a necessary rather than a sufficient condition for intervention, recognizing that sometimes 'the attempt to exercise control would produce other evils, greater than those which it would prevent' (I. 11). Therefore the mere demonstration that a particular case of speaking or writing is liable to cause harm may not always be enough to warrant its suppression. If the harm principle were construed as providing a sufficient basis for intervention, then the result would be a much more restrictive set of guidelines than Mill would be prepared to countenance. Thus, to cite an example of J.W.N. Watkins, it could plausibly be argued on the basis of the harm principle understood as a sufficient ground for intervention that the series of scientific papers which made possible the construction of the atom-bomb should have been suppressed, given the evident harm that atom-bombs could do.[4] On the same basis, it would seem arbitrary to classify as unacceptable modes of expression, as Mill does, only direct and immediate instigations to commit harmful acts. Far more damage in the long run was caused by the publication of Hitler's *Mein Kampf* than by any number of rabble-rousing speeches of the kind that Mill thinks may be banned. But it is hard to believe that Mill would have approved of the prohibition of Hitler's book by some far-seeing censor of the Weimar Republic. The ideas of *Mein Kampf* may be repellent, but Mill's claim is that bad ideas need to be put on the table rather than swept under it, so that their deficiencies can be exposed in a process of open discussion. That bad ideas may sometimes meet with more success than they deserve is an unfortunate fact of life, yet Mill's view, as we shall see, is that it is a price worth paying for avoiding the various evils associated with the practice of censorship.

II. 3–20: The danger of stifling a true opinion

The first possibility that Mill considers is that an opinion that the authorities seek to suppress 'may possibly be true'. Although those who wish to suppress it deny its truth, they are not infallible. 'To refuse a hearing to an opinion because they are sure that it is false,' writes Mill, 'is to assume that *their* certainty is the same thing as *absolute* certainty. All silencing of discussion is an assumption of infallibility' (II. 3).

Alexander Bain, Mill's friend and biographer, considered that the pages Mill devoted to this position 'show a combination of reasoning and eloquence that has never been surpassed, if indeed ever equalled, in the cause of intellectual freedom'.[5] Mill's essential complaint is that human beings are all-too often lacking in the intellectual humility to admit that they may be wrong, particularly in their most cherished beliefs. Everyone knows himself in principle to be fallible, but too few are inclined to take practical precautions against their own fallibility. Even those who have some experience of being contradicted and of being set right when they are wrong tend to place implicit trust in opinions which have the support of 'the world', or at least of that part of it with which they come into contact: their party, sect, church or class of society (II. 4). The great American judge Learned Hand once remarked that 'The spirit of liberty [is that which] is not too sure that it is right.'[6] Mill would have agreed entirely. He reminds us that whole ages have often been found by later ones to have been wrong in some of their most fundamental beliefs (II. 4). If there is one thing we *can* be sure about, it is that to err is human.

Mill proceeds to rebut an objection to his position (II. 5–6). It might be suggested that when the authorities forbid the propagation of error, they are not really assuming their own infallibility, but simply using their best judgement, as they have to do in all the other decisions they make on behalf of the public. 'Judgement is given to men that they may use it. Because it may be used erroneously, are men to be told that they ought not to use it at all?' (II. 5) Mill's reply to the objection is short and decisive. Of course men and governments must act to the best of their ability, and this requires them to make judgements about the facts. But

> [t]here is the greatest difference between presuming an opinion to be true because, with every opportunity for contesting it, it has not been refuted, and assuming its truth for the purpose of not permitting its refutation (II. 6).

The objectionable assumption of infallibility, in other words, occurs not when people make judgements, but when they refuse to acknowledge that those judgements might be wrong. By rejecting the possibility of their own error, they forget that

> [c]omplete liberty of contradicting and disproving our opinion is the very condition which justifies us in assuming its truth for purposes of action; and on no other terms can a being with human faculties have any rational assurance of being right (II. 6).

The emphasis that Mill lays here on the value of discussion and debate reflects one of his own most profoundly held convictions, namely that truth is most likely to emerge when there is a free market in ideas. (To be consistent, Mill must admit that this view, too, might be wrong; but he retains the moral advantage over his opponents that, even if it is, he is allowing his opponents' views to be heard; their rival, anti-libertarian conceptions remain on the table, to be examined by anyone with a mind to do so). When it comes to determining the truth, many heads are better than one. John Skorupski rightly comments that, for Mill, '[a]rguing and assessing evidence is a collective pursuit', and he plausibly identifies this as 'the deepest stratum in Mill's discussion'.[7]

Why is it, asks Mill, that 'there is on the whole a preponderance among mankind of rational opinions and rational conduct'? Not, to be sure, because of 'the inherent force of the human understanding'. Scarcely one person in a hundred is very good at judging any truths which are not self-evident. True belief, rather, arises from a *process* in which mistakes are rectified in the course of time by discussion and experience. The only reliable manner of acquiring knowledge on a subject is 'by hearing what can be said about it by persons of every variety of opinion, and studying all modes in which it can be looked at by every character of mind' (II. 7). Wise people gain their wisdom not by relying on the power of their own unaided intellect but by comparing their opinions with those of other people, and seeing what those others have to say against them. In short, '[t]he beliefs which we have most warrant for have no safeguard to rest on but a standing invitation to the whole world to prove them unfounded' (II. 8). However certain we feel that an opinion is true, we may not place an unqualified credence in it so long as there are others who would dispute it (II. 9).

Sometimes, Mill says, people claim 'not so much that their opinions are true as that they should not know what to do without them', and that their importance to society justifies government in eliminating all rivals. In the case of such opinions that are 'useful, not to say indispensable, to well-being', the claim is that 'something less than infallibility may ... warrant, and even bind, governments to act on their own opinion confirmed by the general opinion of mankind'. Examples of such allegedly 'indispensable' beliefs are the beliefs in God and in a future state or 'any of the commonly received doctrines of morality'. Since, it is said, only bad men 'would desire to weaken these salutary beliefs', there can be no good objection to 'restraining bad men and prohibiting what such men would wish to practise' (II. 10).

A view of the sort that Mill had in mind was defended in the middle of the twentieth century by the British judge Lord Patrick

Devlin in his highly controversial book *The Enforcement of Morals* (1965). According to Devlin, 'It is generally accepted that some shared morality, that is some common agreement about what is right and what is wrong, is an essential element in the constitution of any society.'[8] While Devlin may be right that *some* measure of agreement in moral judgements is vital to the maintenance of social bonds (though there is room for debate on how much agreement is needed, and on what issues), he went on to draw from his sociological premise a much more questionable anti-libertarian conclusion:

There is disintegration when no common morality is observed and history shows that the loosening of moral bonds is often the first stage of disintegration, *so that society is justified in taking the same steps to preserve its moral code as it does to preserve its government and other essential institutions.*[9]

Writing at a time of intense public discussion in Britain about the projected repeal of laws banning homosexual relations between consenting males, Devlin argued that any change in this direction would greatly imperil the social fabric and sap people's faith in the law. If the law was to be respected, it 'must base itself on Christian morals and to the limit of its ability enforce them'.[10] Since society could not live without morals, it followed that even immoral acts which harmed no one else should be punished. Allowing people to sin freely, even in private, placed the very survival of the nation in danger. In what he doubtless took to be a clinching argument, Devlin asked his readers to consider how a nation whose morality had gone soft could have stood up to Hitler and the Nazi hordes twenty-five years earlier: 'A nation of debauchees would not in 1940 have responded satisfactorily to Churchill's call for blood and toil and sweat and tears.'[11]

A view like Devlin's is anathema to Mill. Anyone who claims that such-and-such beliefs or principles are essential to the well-ordering of society, and that any rivals must be stamped out, is setting himself up, Mill says, as an infallible judge of what is vital to social interests; whereas, '[t]he usefulness of an opinion is itself matter of opinion – as disputable, as open to discussion, and requiring discussion as much as the opinion itself' (II. 10). No one is entitled to assume that he is never wrong in assigning opinions to the categories of the socially essential or the socially disastrous. Besides, argues Mill, '[t]he truth of an opinion is part of its utility', since 'no belief which is contrary to truth can be really useful'; so we cannot know whether it is desirable that a proposition should be believed unless we employ the usual methods to determine whether it is true. In the absence of free discussion, we are simply not in a position to say which beliefs are the genuinely useful ones (II. 10).

Mill repeatedly stresses that no matter how sure we feel about something, we make a spurious claim to infallibility if we undertake to decide the question for others (II. 11). We should never try to force our solemn convictions on our neighbours. Perhaps our neighbours are closer to the truth than we are. History is full of instances of the law being employed 'to root out the best men and the noblest doctrines' in the name of piety or morality. As dramatic illustrations of the condemnation of the virtuous by the self-righteous, Mill singles out the cases of Socrates and Jesus (II. 12–13). Those who were responsible for Christ's death were not bad men 'but rather the contrary; men who possessed in a full, or somewhat more than a full measure, the religious, moral, and patriotic feelings of their time and people' (II. 13). Their main fault was to be too sure of themselves.

Mill pays especial attention to the tragic case of the second-century persecution of Christians by the Roman emperor Marcus Aurelius, a man of outstanding virtue and enlightenment and a leading philosopher of the Stoic school (II. 14–15). Conceiving that society was sustained 'by belief and reverence of the received deities' of the traditional Roman pantheon, Marcus Aurelius considered it his duty to extirpate the new religion which threatened to dissolve those supports. And thus, as Mill observes, '[t]his man, a better Christian in all but the dogmatic sense of the word than almost any of the ostensibly Christian sovereigns who have since reigned, persecuted Christianity' (II. 14). Part of Mill's purpose in citing this example is to show how even the best of people can make mistakes when they try to coerce others into believing what they think they should. If someone as wise and as good as Marcus Aurelius could get things so wrong, then so could anyone. But Mill specifically hopes that the example will open the eyes of those contemporary Christians who wish to see their own views enforced and atheism put down. Unless they think of themselves as being wiser and better than the emperor, they should 'abstain from that assumption of . . . infallibility' (II. 14).

Mill takes the opportunity to refute what he regards as the specious and dangerous doctrine that truth benefits from persecution, and that religious intolerance is really a good thing in disguise because it functions as a sieve through which genuine truths will finally pass though falsehoods will not (II. 15–17). Even if it were granted that true doctrine had some intrinsic power of survival that false doctrine lacked, Mill suggests that it would be at the very least ungenerous to suppose that the 'authors of such splendid benefits' as the early Christians or the sixteenth-century Protestant reformers 'should be requited by martyrdom, [and] that their reward should be to be dealt with as the vilest of criminals' (II. 16). 'People who defend this mode of treating benefactors', he comments dryly, 'cannot be supposed to set much value on the benefit' (II. 16). But, in any case, 'the dictum that truth always triumphs over persecution is one of those pleasant falsehoods which men repeat after one another till they pass into commonplaces, but which all experience refutes' (II. 17). Mill provides a lengthy list of religious reformers who have been successfully put down along with their doctrines, and draws the historical moral that '[p]ersecution has always succeeded save where the heretics were too strong a party to be effectually persecuted'. The fact is that '[i]t is a piece of idle sentimentality that truth, merely as truth, has any inherent power denied to error of prevailing against the dungeon and the stake. Men are not more zealous for truth than they often are for error . . .' (II. 17). The correct weapons to use against ideas that we believe to be wrong or dangerous are not fire and sword but evidence and argument.

Paragraphs 18 to 20 are devoted to a survey of contemporary attitudes towards the holders of heterodox opinions, especially about religious matters. Mill weighs his society in the balance and finds it sadly wanting. True, mid-Victorian Britain no longer puts to death heretics and those who introduce new opinions. But it would be foolishly complacent to think that intolerance has ceased to exist. The country is not yet 'a place of mental freedom' in which people can voice their opinions without fear of social stigma (II. 19). Indeed, Mill says, we should not flatter ourselves 'that we are yet free from the stain even of legal persecution' (II. 18). As recently as 1857, 'an unfortunate man, said to be of unexceptionable conduct in all relations of life, was sentenced to twenty months' imprisonment for uttering, and writing on a gate, some offensive words concerning Christianity' (II. 18). Mill cites further cases in which individuals who had professed atheistic opinions had been insultingly treated by judges in courts of law or denied proper justice, and he singles out for particular ridicule the prohibition against the admission of evidence in court of anyone who refuses to take the religious oath to tell the truth. As an example of Mill's argumentative style at its most pithy and devastating, this is worth quoting in full:

> The rule . . . is suicidal and cuts away its own foundation. Under pretence that atheists must be liars, it admits the testimony of all atheists who are willing to lie, and rejects only those who brave the obloquy of publicly confessing a detested creed rather than affirm a falsehood. A rule thus self-convicted of absurdity so far as regards its professed purpose can be kept in force only as a badge of hatred, a relic of persecution; a persecution, too, having the peculiarity that the qualification for undergoing it is the being clearly proved not to deserve it. (II. 18)

Yet the real problem, Mill considers, is not such 'rags and remnants' of legal persecution but the 'merely social intolerance' which, though it does not kill or imprison anybody, makes it difficult for those who profess dissentient opinions to obtain social acceptance or advancement. Since the expression of an unpopular opinion can be seriously damaging to a person's reputation or career prospects, it is much safer to keep all such opinions to oneself. But a state of affairs in which 'the most active and inquiring intellects find it advisable to keep the general principles and grounds of their convictions within their own breast' is unhealthy, because it represses moral courage and causes people to become 'either mere conformers to commonplace, or timeservers for truth' (II. 19). Mill skates over how moral courage would be sustained in a situation where no limits whatever were placed on thought and expression – where anyone could say anything at all without fear of negative legal or social repercussions. The need for courage to speak one's mind could hardly exist except where there were penalties for speaking it. However, Mill's main claim in this passage is a powerful and plausible one: that an enforced conformity of thought has a deadening effect on intellectual life and discourages 'free and daring speculation on the highest subjects' (II. 19).

Furthermore, everyone suffers when free thought is repressed, and not just those whose unorthodox opinions are put down. 'The greatest harm done', Mill says, 'is to those who are not heretics, and whose whole mental development is cramped and their reason cowed by the fear of heresy.' Controversy is good for all since it stimulates not just the advanced thinkers but also 'persons of the most ordinary intellect' to think outside the conventional boxes. The present day and age, however, is doing its best to stamp out all controversy on important questions, and to ensure a mentally stultifying uniformity of thought (II. 20). Or so Mill maintains. As we have already seen, not all of Mill's contemporaries were so convinced that the times were antagonistic to the challenging of the old and the offering of new opinions. And it is worth recalling in this context that *On Liberty* was not the only great book to issue from British presses in the year 1859. Another was Charles Darwin's *On the Origin of Species by Means of Natural Selection*.

II.21–33: *The value of confronting truth with falsity*
Mill now moves on to the second division of his argument. Even if received ideas happen to be true, it is still a very good thing to make them stand up for themselves and do battle with rival ideas. For, however true an opinion may be, 'if it is not fully, frequently, and fearlessly discussed, it will be held as a dead dogma, not a living truth' (II. 21). There is little to be said for holding a view – even a true one – if we cannot defend it against challenges and say why it should be preferred to the alternatives. This, says Mill, 'is not the way in which truth ought to be held by a rational being'. Indeed, a true belief held in this way is really no better than a superstition (II. 22).

Mill's claim that as rational beings we ought to know *why* we believe what we do has strong echoes of John Milton's contention in his *Areopagitica* (1644) that 'faith and knowledge thrives by exercise'. Milton's celebrated tract in favour of press freedom was published in the third year of the English Civil War between King Charles I and Parliament, when each side was extremely anxious to put its own spin on the course of events and a variety of religious denominations and sects strove to have the dominant voice. 'A man may be a heretic in the truth', wrote Milton; 'and if he believe things only because his Pastor says so, or the Assembly so determines, without knowing other reason, though his belief be true, yet the very truth he holds, becomes his heresy'. Scripture has compared truth to a streaming fountain; yet 'if her waters flow not in a perpetual progression, they sicken into a muddy pool of conformity and tradition'.[12]

This is precisely Mill's view. Except in the sole case of mathematics, where 'there is nothing at all to be said on the wrong side of the question', we cannot claim to hold an opinion rationally unless we have some idea of why it deserves our allegiance more than its rivals (II. 23). Besides, where the grounds of an opinion are forgotten in the absence of discussion, the real meaning of the opinion is very often lost as well:

> The words which convey it cease to suggest ideas, or suggest only a small portion of those they were originally employed to communicate. Instead of a vivid conception and a living belief, there remain only a few phrases retained by rote; or, if any part, the shell and husk of the meaning is retained, the finer essence being lost. (II. 26)

Not only do we not know *why* we hold that opinion, but we scarcely know *what* opinion it is we hold. We pay mere lip-service to a form of words.

Alexander Bain believed that Mill exaggerated the need to keep in mind the opposite of every opinion in order to prevent the opinion from becoming a dead dogma. Admitting that when a view is actively challenged, its defenders are 'put on the *qui vive* in its defence', Bain nonetheless thought that there are plenty of things that we quite reasonably believe without all the time maintaining 'imaginary opponents' to them. For example, '[w]e need not conjure up disbelievers in gravitation so long as a hundred observatories and a hundred thousand ships are constantly at work testing its consequences'.[13]

But this objection, though superficially plausible, is more resistable than Bain imagines. It is true that whenever we throw a ball in the air and see it fall down again, or feel how much more effort it takes to climb a steep hill than descend it, we in effect subject the law of gravity to a critical test. And since all our experience to date has been supportive of the law, there may seem little point in entertaining the possibility that it might suddenly cease to hold. But it is a point of logic that although no amount of positive instances can ever make a law-like statement absolutely certain, only one negative instance is sufficient to falsify it. Therefore it is sound scientific practice to attempt to discover conditions which *falsify* the principles that are believed to be laws. By 'looking for trouble' in this way, rather than by endlessly repeating experiments which appear to confirm their hypotheses, scientists are more likely to come across evidence which compels them to revise and so improve their theories. The use of such 'falsificationist' methodology and, more broadly, the entertainment of alternative theoretical options, have led to many striking advances in scientific knowledge over the last couple of centuries: exactly as Mill would have predicted.

Scientific theories commonly have to struggle against rival theories, and the proponents of one theory may have a long and hard battle on their hands before they can show conclusively that the opposing views are false (II. 23). By contrast, those who hold a religious belief, e.g. that Christ is divine or that God is composed of three persons, believe something which is incapable of verification or falsification by experience or experiment. But this does not mean that they are entitled to maintain their belief unchallenged. The least that can be expected of religious believers is that they should listen to criticism of and consider the alternatives to their position. If they refuse, then they believe in an essentially blinkered way and their belief is to all intents and purposes a 'superstition' (Mill) or a 'heresy' (Milton).

On the view which Mill shares with Milton, then, we know little of a matter unless we know it from all sides:

> He who knows only his own side of the case knows little of that. His reasons may be good, and no one may have been able to refute them. But if he is equally unable to refute the reasons on the opposite side, if he does not so much as know what they are, he has no ground for preferring either opinion. (II. 23)

But granting the importance of subjecting opinions to critical tests and the trials of debate, is it necessary that *everyone* who holds them should know all that can be said for and against them? Not everyone has much skill in engaging with 'the mis-statements or fallacies of an ingenious opponent'; so would it not be better for theologians and philosophers to undertake the task on behalf of everyone else? People who lack the knowledge or the ability to resolve every intellectual difficulty for themselves may then trust to authority for their beliefs, and rest secure in the knowledge that all the difficulties that have been raised 'have been or can be answered by those who are specially trained to the task' (II. 24). Furthermore, if people are told what to believe, then they will desist from making ill-informed objections to matters they don't understand. If men could all be made to have true opinions, James Fitzjames Stephen was to write a few years later, it would be 'the greatest of all intellectual blessings'.[14]

Mill devotes several pages to refuting this view, which shows how seriously he takes it. And this is hardly surprising – since he had defended precisely this position himself in an earlier phase of his career! In his essay 'Civilization', published in 1836, Mill complained that the world contained too many books that were hastily written and even more hastily read, with the sad result that 'the world ... gorges itself with intellectual food, and in order to swallow the more, *bolts* it'.[15] At that time Mill thought that the best remedy would be for 'the leading intellects of the age' to combine for the purpose of passing judgement on new publications, so that those of real merit should 'come forth with the stamp on them from the first, of the approval of those whose names would carry authority'.[16] A little later (1840), in an essay on the poet and philosopher Coleridge, Mill expressed considerable enthusiasm for Coleridge's proposal for the formation of a *clerisy*, a collection of wise and learned individuals who would function as arbiters of ideas and guides to truth for the general public.[17]

By 1859, Mill had wholly abandoned the view that a set of experts could safely be entrusted with the task of being intellectual mentors and teachers for the rest of society. Specialist areas of knowledge, of course, require specialist expertise, and Mill does not object to our deferring to the authority of those who know more than we do about some technical subject-matter. It would be foolish for a person without proper training to attempt to dispute with geologists the origins of earthquakes or with oncologists the causes of cancer. (This consideration suggests a possibility that Mill misses, namely that there is an argument under the harm principle for government protection of the public against those who try to sell expensive wonder-drugs or health-foods by making fraudulent claims for their efficacy which non-experts are in no position to evaluate). But we should be reluctant to take on trust from any self- or publicly-appointed 'experts' advice on how to live our lives, or on what moral or political values we ought to hold, or on what religious creed we should follow. These are matters to be debated in the market-place, openly and by everyone.

To support his case that as many people as possible, and not just an intellectual elite, should be involved in discussion and debate in these areas, Mill offers two minor arguments and then a more significant consideration. The first argument is an *ad hominem* one aimed specifically at members of Protestant churches (and thus, by implication, at the British Establishment). (An *ad hominem* – literally 'to the man' – argument is one that aims to demonstrate some inconsistency or incoherence in the position of a particular adversary). Since Protestants hold that it is up to each individual to decide his or her own religious commitment, they cannot then claim that the responsibility for doing this can be devolved to someone else, such as a pastor or a teacher. The second argument is that books are now so abundant that it would be quite impracticable, even if one thought it desirable in principle, to restrict their perusal to the 'instructed'. For better or worse – and Mill thinks definitely for the better – it is no longer possible to confine the discussion of ideas of general interest within a narrow circle of experts.

But the most important consideration is that people should retain their beliefs in a vibrant and vital condition, and to this end they have to experience those beliefs being constantly challenged and reappraised. The Chinese Communist leader Mao Tse-Tung justified the Cultural Revolution of the 1960s by arguing that a society becomes indolent, feeble and self-complacent once it is allowed to emerge from a state of revolutionary ferment. Mill was no social revolutionary but he did believe that ideas rapidly became weary, stale, flat and unprofitable when they began to be taken for granted. This fate, he thought, had already overtaken contemporary religious belief. In his judgement, many people's religious views were now so inert and spiritless that they no longer had any real connection with 'the inner life of the human being'. In contrast with earlier Christians who maintained their faith with passion, and even gave their lives for it in times of persecution, their modern descendants had mostly forgotten 'all of the belief except the formularies', to which they give but 'a dull and torpid assent' (II. 27).

Religion, Mill suggests, has turned into a mere code of genteel behaviour. While many people still sincerely claim to be Christians, their mode of life has little to do with the simplicity, humility and charity preached by Jesus; in fact it has become so wholly conventional in kind that '[w]henever conduct is concerned, they look round for Mr A and B to direct them how far to go in obeying Christ' (II. 28).

However, Mill's claim that mid-Victorian Christianity was all show and no substance is itself open to challenge. The fierce partisanship which surfaced in so many religious disputes of the day scarcely supports the idea that people regarded religion with indifference – even if some of those disputes (e.g. over the proper furnishing of churches, or whether clergy conducting services should wear surplices or not) may not strike us as having much to do with the central tenets of Christianity. Not everyone heard the words of the gospels, as Mill says they did, as merely 'amiable and bland' (II. 29). Victoria's reign was an era of muscular Christianity in which dedicated men and women worked hard to bring home a religious message that was far from bland to the poor, the needy and the suffering, both in the gloomy industrial cities and further afield, in the ever-expanding empire. Mill is assuredly right that for many Victorians, attending church or chapel was more a matter of demonstrating one's social respectability than saving one's immortal soul; but he over-generalizes in asserting that Christianity is no longer a 'living belief which regulates conduct' (II. 28).

It is unlikely that most of those mid-Victorians for whom Christian belief was still a plant of vigorous growth were especially knowledgeable about theology or familiar with the more searching and abstruse forms of intellectual critique to which religion was being subjected by mid-century. But this does not mean that they lacked stimulants to a lively faith. It was commonly feared that Christianity was increasingly under threat from advanced thinkers who, in the lapidary phrase of the mathematician Laplace, 'had no need of that hypothesis'; it was also patently losing ground among the industrial working class. (The Religious Census of 1851 revealed the startling fact that barely 50 per cent of the total population of England and Wales had attended a church service on Midlent Sunday, and much less than half of the working people of London and other large cities).[18] If Christianity was to retain its traditional ideological and moral pre-eminence, it was clear that it would have to be defended against both scepticism and indifference. For many Victorian Christians, the moment had come to stand up and be counted, to affirm their faith and demonstrate the perennial relevance of the gospels in an age dominated by money and machines. And if existing religious institutions were not suitable for the job, then new ones would have to be invented. Six years after the publication of *On Liberty*, William Booth, a Methodist preacher, set up the Christian Mission to feed and clothe the poor in London's East End. Later, in 1878, the Mission provided the basis of one of the most spectacularly successful of philanthropic Christian enterprises, the Salvation Army. The missionary efforts of Booth and of many other like-minded Christians, from a variety of denominations, hardly indicate a religion that had become, in Mill's words, wholly incrusted and petrified 'against all other influences addressed to the higher parts of our nature' (II. 27). On the other hand, they afford some confirmation of his thesis that beliefs exhibit most vitality when there are forces of opposition to confront them.

If beliefs benefit from being challenged, so too do their holders when they are forced to defend them. Having to justify our beliefs keeps us mentally agile and alert; it is a tonic for our intellectual health. Although Mill lays no great stress on this theme in chapter II of *On Liberty*, it makes its appearance two years later in *Utilitarianism*, where he discusses at some length the nature of happiness. Because human beings possess 'faculties more elevated than the animal appetites', they cannot expect to be truly happy unless they make use of their mental capacities. There is 'no known Epicurean theory of life' (i.e. one that holds that happiness is the proper goal of life), says Mill, 'which does not assign to the pleasures of the intellect, of the feelings and imagination, and of the moral sentiments, a much higher value than those of mere sensation'.[19] And even where mental struggles prove to be more painful than pleasant, the significant fact is that

[f]ew human creatures would consent to be changed into any of the lower animals, for a promise of the fullest allowance of a beast's pleasures; no intelligent human being would consent to be a fool, no instructed person would be an ignoramus, no person of feeling and conscience would be selfish and base, even though

they should be persuaded that the fool, the dunce, or the rascal is better satisfied with his lot than they are.[20]

The claim that using our minds makes us happier individuals readily dovetails into the discussion of *On Liberty* and supplies an additional counter to the idea that the multitude should have their opinions spoon-fed to them by an intellectual elite or clerisy. It is the fool's way to believe something because someone else has told him that he should. If fools are less happy and fulfilled than those who actively employ their minds in searching for truth, then it cannot be good for people to believe in that way.

II. 34–39: The possibility that conflicting opinions may share the truth between them

This third possibility is, Mill thinks, the one most commonly encountered. On most disputed matters, the truth is not all on one side or the other; more often, each member of a pair of conflicting opinions contains a part of the truth, along with some falsehood. Mill does not mean, of course, to deny the logician's Law of Excluded Middle – the principle that a proposition is either true or false but not both. Having written a major treatise on logic, Mill knows that it cannot both be true and not true that today is Tuesday or that $2+2=4$. His claim is rather that the opinions we express typically consist of complexes of propositions, some of which are true and others false. Our knowledge of many matters is partial and imperfect, and we should be tolerant of contrary opinions, which may convey to us aspects of the truth that we have overlooked (II. 34).

Mill provides a number of examples of controversies to show how truth may be divided between two sides, with neither having a monopoly of it. The first is the eighteenth-century dispute between those who 'were lost in admiration of what is called civilization, and of the marvels of modern science, literature, and philosophy', and the followers of the Swiss thinker Jean-Jacques Rousseau (1712–78) who lamented the loss of 'simplicity of life' and complained of 'the enervating and demoralizing effect of the trammels and hypocrisies of artificial society' (II. 35). Both sides, in Mill's view, were right within certain limits, since modern civilization exhibits both the virtues identified by the one and the vices described by the other. In a similar way, the opposing parties of conservatism and reform that dominate contemporary political life can each claim to have grasped a part of the truth. 'Each of these modes of thinking', Mill argues, 'derives its utility from the deficiencies of the other; but it is in a great measure the opposition of the other that keeps each within the limits of reason and sanity' (II. 36).

But it is to Christianity that Mill characteristically turns for his primary example of a partial truth that does not recognize itself to be such. This time the target in his sights is the Christian ethical code, which he controversially describes as 'incomplete and one-sided' (II. 37). Mill displays considerable boldness in taking issue with the substance of Christian morality; even as late as 1859 this risked causing major public shock and outrage. In this portion of *On Liberty*, Mill is not so much defending the right to freedom of expression as exercising it. Even his usually staunch supporter Bain judged Mill to be imprudent in courting the anger of the zealots quite so openly. It was impossible, he thought, that Mill's fault-finding would be viewed dispassionately, since it would inevitably be seen as 'challenging the pretensions of Christianity to be a divine revelation'.[21]

The nub of Mill's objection to the Christian ethic is that it is unreasonably slanted in favour of a passive rather than an active manner of life. Mill makes it clear that the main object of his strictures is not the sacred revelation of the gospels, but the Christian ethic as it has developed over later centuries. Yet even the ethic of Jesus himself comes in for some criticism. Mill contends that this was never intended to form a complete code of morals by itself, and that it needs to be supplemented from other sources (II. 38). Fortunately, 'everything which is excellent in ethics' may consistently be appended to the gospel ethic, the problem with it being not what it contains but what it leaves out. However, while Mill *says* that the problem with Christian moral teaching is that, while correct as far as it goes, it forms only a part of the truth, some of his remarks on Christian ideals gesture towards a deeper dissatisfaction:

> Christian morality (so called) has all the characters of a reaction; it is, in great part, a protest against paganism. Its ideal is negative rather than positive; passive rather than active; innocence rather than nobleness; abstinence from evil rather than energetic pursuit of good; in its precepts (as has been well said) 'thou shalt not' predominates unduly over 'thou shalt'. (II. 37)

Moreover, in its 'horror of sensuality' it has made an idol of asceticism and self-denial; although Mill does not spell out this complaint very clearly, his point is presumably that by placing the major focus on getting to heaven when we die, Christianity unduly disvalues many of the goods of the present life. To complete the indictment, Mill holds that the Christian ethic attempts to motivate us to be moral chiefly by placing before our eyes 'the hope of heaven and the threat of hell', thereby giving to human morality 'an essentially selfish character'. In this regard it falls considerably below the standard set by 'the best of the ancients' (i.e. the Greek philosophers), who taught that we should do our duty by our neighbour for more selfless reasons (II. 37).

Mill's conclusion from his critical discussion is that 'other ethics than any which can be evolved from purely Christian sources must exist side by side with Christian ethics to produce the moral regeneration of mankind' (II. 38). Although he does not elaborate on what those 'other ethics' should be, it is plausible to suppose that he has in mind a combination of Greek (especially Aristotelian) thought about the virtues, and utilitarianism. Both of these are 'this-worldly' philosophies which encourage us to realize the conditions of our personal and social fulfilment in the present life, rather than in some (highly doubtful) existence to come. Their appeal to Mill is also that they promote an active, rather than a passive, form of life, in which we strive to acquire the excellences of character and mind that maximally enrich our own existence while making us most serviceable to others. Bain argues that 'activity in virtue depends quite as much on individual virtue as on creed' (adding that 'the typical Anglo-Saxon when highly virtuous, is almost sure to be actively so').[22] Mill would not have disagreed with this, nor taken it as a criticism. But he would certainly have resisted Bain's implication that such active or 'Anglo-Saxon' virtue is adequately promoted by Christian morality.

Whether Mill presents a fair and accurate outline of the character of Christian ethics is open to debate. One generally sympathetic early reviewer of *On Liberty*, the Anglican clergyman and ecclesiastical historian Richard Church, maintained with some justice that Mill was too inclined to take the narrow Calvinistic or puritan version of Christianity as the type of the whole. This, claimed Church, was to miss the fact that there was 'a larger, more ancient, more human conception of Christian morality than that of so-called

Calvinism'. Mill, he thought, might have been less persuaded that the Christian ideal was merely negative if he had pondered on some words from St Paul's Letter to the Philippians: 'Finally, my brethren, whatsoever things are true, whatsoever things are honest, whatsoever things are just, whatsoever things are lovely, if there be any virtue, and if there be any praise, think on these things.'[23] That Mill had failed to consider the broader and more generous forms of Christian morality Church put down to the fact – which Mill himself would probably have granted – that 'great phenomena are often unrealized, even by the most powerful minds, when foreign to their usual ways of thought and life'.[24]

Mill ends this section of the chapter by raising the question whether 'the most unlimited use of the freedom of enunciating all possible opinions would put an end to the evils of religious or philosophical sectarianism' (II. 39). His candid conclusion is that it would not. Indeed, the tendency of opinions to become sectarian is actually exacerbated, rather than cured, by the habit of free discussion. But this is decidedly the lesser of two evils:

> Not the violent conflict between parts of the truth, but the quiet suppression of half of it, is the formidable evil; there is always hope when people are forced to listen to both sides; it is when they attend only to one that errors harden into prejudices, and truth itself ceases to have the effect of truth by being exaggerated into falsehood. (II. 39)

Truth has no chance of emerging until 'every opinion which embodies any fraction of the truth, not only finds advocates, but is so advocated as to be listened to' (II. 39). Admittedly, the passionate adherents of sects may reap little good from a process of discussion which merely leads them to harden their own prejudices. Yet if the arrogance and delusive certainty of sectarianism are ugly and regrettable, they are a price worth paying for the existence of a free market in ideas. While the 'impassioned partisan' is foolishly content to remain in his blinkered state, the 'calmer and more disinterested bystander' benefits from the opportunity to hear all sides of a question (II. 39).

II. 40–44: Conclusions, and a note on the ethics of debate

Following three short paragraphs (40–43) summarising the conclusions reached so far, Mill introduces one final ethical issue in the
last paragraph of the chapter. Some people, he notes, say that the
free expression of opinions should be permitted only on one condition not yet mentioned, namely that views should always be
presented in a temperate and civil manner, and free from such faults
as invective, sarcasm and the unjust denigration of opponents (II.
44). Mill is sympathetic to the call for honesty and courtesy in
debate, and he strongly condemns those who resort to calumniating
their opponents in order to make up for the deficiencies of their own
arguments. Yet he is firmly against the proposal to enforce an eti-
quette of debate, which he sees as fraught with difficulties.

To begin with, it would be impossible to lay down any rules that
would satisfy everyone, particularly as some people are more thin-
skinned than others and liable to take offence from any hard-
pressed opposition to their own views. (In this connection, we may
consider how, in our own day as in Mill's, some proponents of
religious views regard *any* criticism of their position as blasphemous
and intolerable). Then there is the question of who the arbiters
would be of the bounds between acceptable and unacceptable styles
of debate. (The idea that this could be left in the hands of some
committee of intellectuals is utterly at odds with the spirit of *On
Liberty*). If the defenders of orthodoxy are entrusted with the task,
there is a real danger that they will, wittingly or otherwise, employ
double standards and demand greater restraint and deference from
those who attack, than from those who uphold, conventional opinions. Mill concludes that 'law and authority have no business' in
constraining debate, and that people need to make up their own
minds whether discussion is being conducted properly and fairly.
To this end, they should look out for 'want of candour, or malig-
nity, bigotry, or intolerance of feeling', and they should also be
careful not to infer the presence of these faults from the *side* which a
person takes. The 'real morality of discussion', Mill asserts, is to
give 'merited honour' to those who present their own and their
opponents' views calmly and accurately, and who treat those
opponents with justice and respect (II. 44).

Despite Mill's wise words of caution, some would claim that
practical circumstances do not allow governments of the present
day to stand wholly on the sidelines in regard to how public debate

and discussion on sensitive topics is conducted. Since governments, the argument runs, have a duty to maintain the peace, they may reasonably seek to suppress the publication or dissemination of printed, oral or web-based material that risks giving rise to civil disorder through the offence it will give to certain audiences. When Danish newspapers in 2005 published cartoons that satirised the prophet Mohammed, protest riots occurred in several countries that cost the lives of several people, while one western newspaper editor was murdered by Muslim extremists. In the light of such cases, some political commentators and politicians have suggested that it would be in the public interest for states to ban the publication of any material likely to have a dangerously inflammatory effect on the members of specific religious or ethnic groups.

We can be sure that Mill would have had none of this. While he would deplore the deployment of discourteous methods of debate, cruel satire or deliberately hurtful or demeaning innuendo, he would not approve of government or judicial censorship of published material *except* where it clearly constituted an intentional and immediate incitement to action harmful to others. That the publicization of a particular point of view might cause offence to some groups or individuals is not, for Mill, a sufficient reason to prevent it; for sometimes truth *is* offensive (and we have no right, in any case, never to be offended). Where people have controversial things to say, they should be allowed to say them and then challenged to defend their opinions against objections. (There is no doubt that Mill would have been strongly opposed to the existence in Germany, Austria and some other countries of laws forbidding the denial of the Nazi Holocaust; he would have seen this not only as inconsistent with liberal principles of free speech but as a wasted opportunity to demonstrate, with evidence, the folly of the Holocaust-deniers' position).

We have already noted that Mill does not delineate with the necessary care the boundary between material that incites people to act harmfully against others, and that which sows fear, hatred or contempt in their minds, with potentially harmful later consequences. Yet in his defence it may be said that this is a very difficult boundary to draw. There are two main reasons for this. The first is that it is often very hard to predict with any pretence to accuracy what the long-term results of a particular speech, book or newspaper article are likely to be. (It is probable, for instance, that the Danish cartoons would have produced no more than some minor grumbles had they not been unexpectedly reproduced, for internal political purposes, in a Muslim country). The second is that in a liberal state that values both freedom of expression *and* the preservation of the lives and safety of individuals, it will sometimes be necessary to strike a balance between these values which, though in principle compatible, are capable for contingent reasons of conflicting. Under the harm principle, freedom is rightfully restricted where its exercise threatens to produce harmful consequences for others. Unfortunately, no liberal philosopher has yet come up with a satisfactory general schema for striking this balance, and nor should we hold our breath that one will be forthcoming very soon.

Study Questions

1. Are there any circumstances in which governments may legitimately constrain free speech?
2. Is Mill right to say that those who seek to suppress an opinion they disagree with effectively assume their own infallibility?
3. Does our rationally believing some proposition always require that we should be willing to consider arguments or evidence that we might be wrong?
4. Do conflicting opinions normally 'share the truth between them'?
5. Is Christian morality, as Mill claimed, too negative in its fundamental ideals?
6. What ethical standards should govern the practice of debate and discussion?

CHAPTER III: OF INDIVIDUALITY, AS ONE OF THE ELEMENTS OF WELL-BEING

III. 1: Individuality and happiness

Mill might well have called chapter III of *On Liberty*, 'In Praise of Individuality'. Literally and figuratively at the centre of the book, it provides the most sustained defence of 'the leading thought' of the work, namely, 'the importance, to man and society, of a large variety in types of character, and of giving full freedom to human nature to expand itself in innumerable and conflicting directions'.[1]

Mill modestly disclaimed the credit of saying anything very original in the chapter, preferring to describe it as restating a truth which, 'though in many ages confined to insulated thinkers, mankind have probably at no time since the beginning of civilization been entirely without'.[2] But he thought that the importance of reiterating this truth in the mid-nineteenth century could hardly be overstated. For this was an age – or so he claimed – that was particularly antagonistic to any departures by individuals from the conventional norms. In Mill's pessimistic view, people were coming more and more to resemble one another: 'Comparatively speaking, they now read the same things, listen to the same things, see the same things, go to the same places, have their hopes and fears directed to the same objects, have the same rights and liberties, and the same means of asserting them' (III. 18). Individuality as a mode of existence was in considerable danger of becoming extinct.

Mill, who always gave credit where credit was due, acknowledged the profound influence on his own thinking of the part-contemporary German liberal thinker Wilhelm von Humboldt (1767–1835), even borrowing some lines from the older writer to form the epigraph of *On Liberty*:

> The grand, leading principle, towards which every argument unfolded in these pages directly converges, is the absolute and essential importance of human development in its richest diversity.

These words come from von Humboldt's most important book, first published in German in 1792 and translated into English in 1854 as *The Sphere and Duties of Government*. Mill was impressed not only by von Humboldt's stirring defence of the value of human differences, and his proposal that we should engage in 'experiments in living' (echoed in *On Liberty* at III. 1), but by his conception of liberty as the essential condition for personal development. According to the German author:

> The true end of Man, or that which is prescribed by the eternal and immutable dictates of reason, and not suggested by vague and transient desires, is the highest and most harmonious development of his powers to a complete and consistent whole. Freedom is the grand and indispensable condition which the possibility of such a development presupposes; ...[3]

Mill believed that the freedom to develop one's character, talents and interests according to one's own blueprint was being sapped by the conditions of modern civilization, with their increasing pressure to live as others do and to fall in with 'the general arrangements of society'. His fears about the deadening effects of contemporary social arrangements on personal development were already well in evidence in his essay 'Civilization' of 1836, where he complained of 'the relaxation of individual energy: or rather, the concentration of it within the narrow sphere of the individual's money-getting pursuits'.[4] Modern civilization, he conceded, had its good points: it had led to a welcome 'increase in humanity, a decline in bigotry, as well of arrogance and the conceit of caste, among our conspicuous classes'. Many people were more comfortable, secure and prosperous than ever before. But the downside was that 'by the natural growth of civilization, power passes from individuals to masses, and the weight and importance of an individual, as compared with the mass, sink into greater and greater insignificance'.[5] Under the tyranny of the majority, it was hard to be oneself.

In Wendy Donner's words, '*On Liberty* is an impassioned plea for the liberty that will promote the individuality required for self-development and for the appreciation of more valuable pleasures and pursuits.'[6] As we have seen, Mill makes clearer in *Utilitarianism* than *On Liberty* that the development of personal excellences of character and mind, and the appreciation of what he there terms the 'higher' mental pleasures, are essential ingredients of happiness (happiness, that is, properly so called, as distinct from mere sensory gratification). 'Human beings', Mill writes, 'have faculties more elevated than the animal appetites, and when once made conscious of them, do not regard anything as happiness which does not include their gratification.'[7] It is reasonable to see the promotion of self-development in *On Liberty* as intimately connected with Mill's utilitarian project of enhancing human happiness. If as many people as possible are to be maximally happy, then it is imperative that society allows them sufficient room to discover and develop their capacities, in their own time and their own way.

Mill opens the chapter with a reminder of the harm principle: '[t]he liberty of the individual must be thus far limited; he must not make himself a nuisance to other people'. Thus agents should not 'without justifiable cause do harm to others', either directly, through their own acts, or by inciting third parties to harmful behaviour. Provided that a person refrains from 'molesting others in what concerns them', he should then be left free 'without molestation, to carry his opinions into practice at his own cost'. And this should be seen not just as a right to be grudgingly granted, but as a highly valuable good. It is vital that people should attempt different 'experiments of living' and that 'free scope should be given to varieties of character'. If people are forced to conform all the time to the traditions and customs that others have laid down, then 'one of the principal ingredients of human happiness' is missing, as well as the 'chief ingredient of individual and social progress' (III. 1).

III. 2–9: The importance of individuality to well-being

In the next few paragraphs, Mill sets out his understanding of individuality, and the reasons for its importance, in greater depth. One of the major obstacles that needs to be overcome is the prevailing general indifference to the value of individuality. 'Individual spontaneity', he remarks, 'is hardly recognized by the common modes of thinking as having any intrinsic worth' whatever. Most people, 'being satisfied with the ways of mankind as they now are (for it is they who make them what they are), cannot comprehend why those ways should not be good enough for everybody'. Far too few persons share – or even comprehend – von Humboldt's inspiring vision of the purpose of man as being 'the highest and most harmonious development of his powers to a complete and consistent whole' (III. 2).

Mill concedes that no one asserts that it would be a good thing for people to be *exactly* like one another in their character and conduct. But the contentious issue is the degree to which variety is desirable, and Mill thinks that most people are satisfied with far too little of it. Of course, it would be foolish for a person, in choosing his or her own course in life, to disregard the previous experience of mankind. Mill acknowledges that people have much to learn from one another, and that we all need to be 'taught and trained in youth ... to know and benefit by the ascertained results of human experience'. Nonetheless:

it is the privilege and proper condition of a human being, arrived at the maturity of his faculties, to use and interpret experience in his own way. It is for him to find out what part of recorded experience is properly applicable to his own circumstances and character. (III. 3)

Customs and traditions may provide some useful guidance in this process; but individuals still need to appraise their rightness and wisdom, and decide how relevant they are to their own case. Here we can see, starkly highlighted, Mill's conception of autonomous individuals who assume full responsibility for their own beliefs and actions. 'He who does anything because it is the custom', says Mill, 'makes no choice.' And 'if the grounds of an opinion are not con- clusive to the person's own reason, his reason cannot be strength- ened, but is likely to be weakened, by his adopting it' (III. 3). Indeed:

> [h]e who lets the world, or his own portion of it, choose his plan of life for him has no need of any other faculty than the ape-like one of imitation. He who chooses his plan for himself employs all his faculties. He must use observation to see, reasoning and judgement to foresee, activity to gather materials for decision, discrimination to decide, and when he has decided, firmness and self-control to hold to his deliberate decision. (III. 4)

Human nature, Mill continues, is not a machine to be built according to a model, but more like a tree, which will grow and develop according to the inward forces which make it a living thing – if it is allowed to. In a plain echo of Aristotle, Mill observes that it matters 'not only what men do, but also what manner of men they are that do it'. For '[a]mong the works of man which human life is rightly employed in perfecting and beautifying, the first in importance surely is man himself' (III. 4).

At this point, Mill anticipates a possible objection. Some might think that it is all very well to encourage people to act energetically on their own desires and impulses, but worry what the results of this might be in the case of agents whose desires and impulses are directed towards bad ends. For this reason, strong impulses have traditionally been regarded as 'a peril and a snare', and self- restraint, rather than self-expression, has been seen as virtuous. (Mill does not add, but he might have done, that strong-willed people are also likely to dominate and overpower their weaker neighbours).

Mill's response to the objection (III.5–6) is sketchy and un-satisfactory. He starts by pointing out that there is 'no natural connection between strong impulses and a weak conscience' (III. 5). While this is true, it still leaves the problem of what to do about those people who combine a strong nature with a weak moral sense – that is, wilful agents who either do not recognize or who feel little loyalty to any moral constraints. Mill tries to improve on this answer by urging that strong natures are capable of producing more good than weak ones; but the effect of this is immediately undermined by his candid admission that they may also be capable of more evil (III. 5). He also suggests that '*more good may . . . be made of an energetic nature than of an indolent and impassive one*', and that '*cultivated feelings *may be made the strongest*' in those who have most natural feeling (III. 5; my emphases). But these suggestions raise the obvious question of who is supposed to control the process of improvement. If – as the wording seems to hint – the idea is that others should intervene in the strong-willed agent's life and seek to make him into a better person, with finer or more appropriate feelings, then Mill's position has become self-contradictory.

A person 'whose desires and impulses are not his own', says Mill, 'has no character, no more than a steam engine has a character' (III. 5). Under the harm principle, an agent may be forcibly prevented from doing harm to his neighbours. But Mill, in an almost Nietzschean passage, repeats his opposition to the practice, which he thinks has been far too common in the past, of seeking to govern the character of 'men of strong bodies or minds' who are reluctant to obey the social rules (III. 6).[8] Where such interference succeeds in substituting for his existing desires and impulses other, more socially acceptable ones, then it effectively robs the strong person of his character. Yet we may reasonably question Mill's consistency in refusing to countenance any kind of forcible retraining or other means of cultivating finer feelings in people whose strong desires and impulses make them a threat to other members of society. If their harmful *acts* may be interfered with under the harm principle, then why not too their harmful *characters*? For Mill, the value of individuality is simply too great for any tampering with a person's character to be acceptable. But this raises two obvious questions. The first is whether just *any* individual character should be regarded as valuable. Is it good to have a personality strongly disposed towards the torturing of people or animals, or the rape of children, or the unscrupulous exploitation of everyone else in one's own interests? Were Hitler or the Marquis de Sade better men for having distinctive personalities, with very strong impulses towards the harming of others? The second question is whether Mill's *laissez-faire* attitude to personal character is compatible with the concern that a utilitarian ought to have for the serious harms to others that are likely to flow from people with bad characters. Mill constantly justifies the value he places on individuality by citing the *good* that can be done by people with a strong personality, if they are left to their own devices. Yet this conveniently, and unrealistically, overlooks the *evil* that some people of strong character are equally ready to do.

Mill's final reply to the objection is to suggest that the problem, if it ever was one, is one no longer, since 'society has now got the better of individuality; and the danger which threatens human nature is not the excess, but the deficiency, of personal impulses and preferences' (III. 6). The snag with this line (leaving aside its dubious appraisal of the current situation) is that it implicitly concedes that there might be a problem if a new age of individuality were to dawn. Since Mill is doing his best in *On Liberty* to bring about that dawn, he is entitled to dismiss the worry as unimportant only in so far as he presupposes his own failure.

Mill acknowledges that Victorian people are not devoid of desires and inclinations. But the trouble is that there is nothing individual or spontaneous about these: in Mill's vivid phrase, 'they like in crowds'. It is not even as though they choose what is customary in preference to their own inclinations; Mill's deeper complaint is that '[i]t does not occur to them to have any inclination except for what is customary' (III. 6). So great has become the grip of convention that people

> exercise choice only among things commonly done; peculiarity of taste, eccentricity of conduct are shunned equally with crimes, until by dint of not following their own nature they have no nature to follow: their human capacities are withered and starved: they become incapable of any strong wishes or native pleasures, and are generally without either opinions or feelings of home growth, or properly their own (III. 6).

Mill ascribes some of the responsibility for this state of affairs to the negative influence of Calvinism. This austere form of

Christianity, which had first arrived in Britain from Geneva in the mid-sixteenth century, had given rise to the Puritanism of the Elizabethan and earlier Stuart periods and subsequently retained its position as a major strand in English Protestantism. Mill disliked it heartily. On his construal of its moral doctrine, Calvinism sees 'the one great offence of man' as self-will. Holding human nature to be radically corrupt, Calvinists believe that the only good of which humanity is capable consists in obedience to the will of God. And unfortunately (in Mill's view), even people who do not consider themselves Calvinists are frequently tainted by its ungenerous attitudes towards all human impulses, believing desires to be free of sin only when they are strictly in accordance with the prescriptions of authority (III. 7).

Mill considers Calvinism's 'narrow theory of life' to be not just ethically repugnant but theologically absurd. The 'pinched and hidebound type of character' which it patronises cannot possibly be what a good God would wish to see in us:

> Many persons ... sincerely think that human beings thus cramped and dwarfed are as their Maker designed them to be ... But if it be any part of religion to believe that man was made by a good Being, it is more consistent with that faith to believe that this Being gave all human faculties that they might be cultivated and unfolded, not rooted out and consumed, and that he takes delight in every nearer approach made by his creatures to the ideal conception embodied in them, every increase in any of their capabilities of comprehension, of action, or of enjoyment (III. 8).

Greek philosophy, by contrast, has a quite different (and, Mill clearly implies, much more inspiring) view of human excellence, holding that human nature is bestowed on us 'for other purposes than merely to be abnegated' (i.e. denied and subdued). But neither the Greeks nor Mill recommend that we should follow our spontaneous impulses wherever they lead. While we should not deny our nature, we should aim to exercise self-restraint and govern, rather than be governed by, our passions. Liberty is not the same as licence, and the pursuit of personal excellence should not be confused with self-indulgence. In considering some possible models for us to emulate, Mill warns us against following the example of the brilliant but corrupt Greek soldier and politician Alcibiades (c.450–404 BC), who became a legend in his own lifetime for his ambition, unscrupulous treachery and dissolute living. But nor should we aim to imitate John Knox (c.1513–72), the stern, unbending leader of Scottish Calvinism. If we are seeking an ideal, a far better choice would be the wise, urbane and virtuous Athenian statesman Pericles (c.495–429 BC) (III. 8). Elsewhere, Mill describes Pericles as a person of 'lofty spirit and practical wisdom', 'eminent in all the acquirements, talents, and accomplishments of his country', and a politician who maintained his ascendancy 'solely by his commanding qualities'.[9] In *On Liberty* he represents the type of the individualist who develops his mental and moral excellences to the highest degree, and whose contribution to society is the greater because it is distinctively his.

'In proportion to the development of his individuality', writes Mill, 'each person becomes more valuable to himself, and is, therefore, capable of being more valuable to others'. Such a person lives more fully, 'and when there is more life in the units there is more in the mass which is composed of them'. The most notable ages known to history are those which have fostered the growth of individuality. And 'whatever crushes individuality is despotism, by whatever name it is called and whether it professes to be enforcing the will of God or the injunctions of men' (III.9).

III. 10–13: The value of individuals to society

Some people, Mill points out, have no desire for the kind of liberty necessary for self-development and find it hard to understand why anyone else should want it. For their sake, and so that they do not seek to hinder the freedom of others, Mill thinks it advisable to say more about the social benefits of individuality (III. 10).

One of these is that individuals provide the element of originality that every society requires if it is to avoid stagnation. There is a perennial need, says Mill, for people to make fresh discoveries, to correct old mistakes, and to 'commence new practices and set the example of more enlightened conduct and better taste and sense in human life' (III. 11). Only those who are foolish enough to believe that the world has already achieved perfection will deny this. Of course, not everyone (not even every cultivated individual) is capable of making an original contribution, since to do this requires the further attribute of genius. But while genius is rare, those who possess it are 'the salt of the earth', as they not only 'introduce good things which did not before exist' but 'keep the life in those which already exist'. Geniuses may be few in number but their contribution to the social good is enormous. It is therefore essential to maintain the conditions in which their unique qualities can flourish. And for genius to breathe freely, Mill argues, there has to be 'an *atmosphere* of freedom' (III. 11).

Mill further suggests that geniuses are by definition ('*ex vi terminorum*') 'more individual than any other people', and so less able to fit themselves easily into the usual 'moulds which society provides in order to prevent its members the trouble of forming their own character' (III. 11). Geniuses, in other words, are liable to be eccentric – and such eccentricity can go down badly with commonplace people who dislike personalities or lifestyles that are out of the ordinary. But, in a striking image, Mill remarks that 'one should not complain of the Niagara river for not flowing smoothly between its banks like a Dutch canal' (III. 11).

One might quibble with Mill's account of genius that not all possessors of brilliantly original minds are particularly eccentric in character or demeanour. Mill does not pause to define his notion of genius with any precision, nor does he give any examples of men and women whom he considers fall into the category. However, there is little justification for presuming that anyone who thinks unusual thoughts must also have an unusual personality or lifestyle. If the minds of geniuses are like Niagara rivers, their lives often bear more resemblance to Dutch canals. Mill's remark, at III. 13, that the fact '[t]hat so few now dare to be eccentric marks the chief danger of the time' suggests, rather implausibly, that personal oddity is a good thing in itself. Whether an individual's personal idiosyncrasies are valuable or not must depend on what those features are, not simply on their being idiosyncratic. Yet to quarrel with Mill on this score is to risk missing his main and more persuasive point, that society should not endanger the development or the expression of genius by imposing constraints on the ways in which people may live their lives. Genius must be allowed 'to unfold itself freely both in thought and in practice', or else it will wither (III. 12).

There are very few people, Mill says, who value genius as it deserves. They think it a fine thing for a person to produce a striking poem or picture, but they are uninterested in originality in thought or action. On Mill's analysis, this indifference is yet another regrettable effect of modern civilization, which values human beings in the mass but not as individuals. The result is that individuals are lost in the crowd and 'collective mediocrity' reigns (III. 13). Yet since 'all wise or noble things' owe their origins to individuals and not to the generality, a society that fails to cultivate individuality risks extinguishing the vital creative spark. Ordinary people, given suitable leads, are capable of following them to good effect. But they need to be given the leads. Mill is careful to explain that he is not looking for the kind of hero who seeks to impose his own will on others (this is probably a side-swipe at Thomas Carlyle's praise of such a figure in his *On Heroes, Hero-Worship, and the Heroic in History* [1841]). What are required are individuals who will occupy 'the higher eminences of thought' and inspire others by their teaching and example.

Mill returns to the theme of the social costs of the loss of individuality in a book published shortly after *On Liberty*, the *Considerations on Representative Government* of 1861. There he makes it clear that it is not only modern representative democracy that has proved itself unsympathetic to individuality. History provides other cautionary examples of societies that have attained a high level of civilization and then become frozen in their tracks:

> The Egyptian hierarchy, the paternal despotism of China, were very fit instruments for carrying those nations to the point of civilisation which they attained. But having reached that point, they were brought to a permanent halt for want of mental liberty and individuality; requisites of improvement which the institutions that had carried them thus far entirely incapacitated them from acquiring; and as the institutions did not break down and give place to others, further improvement stopped.[10]

To these examples of stagnating societies *On Liberty* joins a further one, that of the medieval Byzantine Empire, in which Mill claims civilisation had not merely stalled but died out (a judgement, incidentally, not likely to be endorsed by most present-day students of Byzantium) (III. 11). The general moral we are meant to draw from these instances of arrested development is that what has happened before can easily happen again.

However, Mill's gloomy prognostications are open to challenge on two counts. The first is that his idea of what constitutes a flourishing civilization is much more culturally specific than he admits, or realizes. For all Mill's criticism of contemporary norms and his fear of pervasive mediocrity, he is quintessentially Victorian in his assumption that flourishing societies are ones that continuously *progress* and *improve*. Yet this is a questionable assumption – and it would doubtless have been contested by many thoughtful representatives of Chinese, Egyptian or Byzantine civilization, if they could have joined in the discussion. Mill thought of these cultures as having got stuck in a rut from which they made no attempt to climb out. But their defenders could have pointed out how very rich a rut it was they occupied. If Mill was appalled by what he saw as the cultural stasis that had endured in China for over two thousand years, a typical Chinese intellectual of the nineteenth century would have cited the continuous production through that time of first-rate poetry and philosophy, painting and music, and of the maintenance of a stable social structure while Europe was relatively poor, politically fragmented and chronically riven by violent disorder. (The same intellectual might have added that genius does not necessarily have to manifest itself in the creation of things that are utterly new and unexpected; it can find an outlet, too, in working fresh variations on old themes). Moreover, progress, as we can nowadays see better than the Victorians could, can exact its own heavy price. The last two hundred years of 'progressive' western civilization have caused more problems and dangers for the planet – to the point of jeopardizing the survival of mankind – than did the previous two millennia of Chinese civilization. Civilization of the kind that Mill admired has turned out to be a very mixed blessing, and the case for progressive rather than static cultures is less assured than he believed.

Second, Mill undoubtedly overestimated the threat to individuality, and the consequent danger of stagnation, posed by a modern commercial democratic society. The massive political, economic, social, artistic and technological changes that have occurred since 1859 hardly support Mill's thesis that mid-Victorian culture was in imminent danger of shedding the spirit of enterprise and innovation. It is true that we can only say this with the benefit of a hindsight that was unavailable to him. But many of his own contemporaries were not persuaded that the age of individuality was past. Nor is it easy to see why Mill was so convinced that the times were inhospitable to individuality and genius when we consider the highly original men and women who occupied the mid-Victorian stage: Darwin, Huxley, Dickens, George Eliot, the Brontë sisters, Tennyson, Brunel, Ruskin, the Arnolds, Rossetti, Disraeli, Gladstone, Florence Nightingale, Newman, Burton, Livingstone and Mill himself, to name but a few.

The shrewd and perceptive Richard Church, writing in 1860, was in no doubt that Mill's picture of individuality involved in a losing battle with custom was 'but a partially true representation of what is'. In Church's opinion, '[t]he current which runs through society is neither so uniform nor so irresistible as he makes it', and there was ample scope for the expression of contrasting views on a vast variety of subjects. 'Such a state of things', he reflected, 'is consistent with much respect for custom, but it is inconceivable without also a large amount of activity of mind and resistance to custom.' Church rejected Mill's view of 'a prevailing servility and submission to intimidation'. Rather, there was much public admiration for 'the bold, enterprising, self-reliant qualities of character', which were much less under threat than Mill imagined.[11] Church also believed that 'in this country, thinkers *are* their own masters, at least to a much greater extent than Mr Mill seems to admit'.[12]

Another, anonymous, reviewer of *On Liberty*, writing in the same year, agreed, though with some reservations about the quality of the output of many of the thinkers of the age. Never before, in this reviewer's opinion, had there been 'an epoch distinguished by a greater *flush* of opinions, even the most reckless and absurd'. Indeed, it had become almost impossible to 'see the "green ground" in Truth's meadow for the dandelions, thistles, and poppies that have sprung up in it'. There was no need for Mill to worry about the restriction of individual opinion when the times were witnessing an explosion of speculation, much of it pseudo-philosophy of the most eccentric kind. In this writer's view, it was 'droll' for Mill to speak about the repression of thought (or what passed for such) when the public was forced to suffer such absurdities as Mormonism, spirit-rapping and clairvoyance.[13]

III. 14: The praise of pluralism (1): Choosing one's own life
In the final pages of chapter III Mill introduces few new ideas but extends and deepens his analysis of the value of individuality and of the threats it faces. The discussion can be read as a sustained apology for a pluralist conception of human well-being which

values diversity of character and heterogeneous lifestyles, and which recommends the making of 'experiments in living' in preference to conforming to any particular ideal of the good life. As Mill puts it, '[t]here is no reason that all human existence should be constructed on one or some small number of patterns' (III. 14). Good lives can take many different forms, and the world is a richer and better place for containing a large variety of lives.

Mill stresses that it is not only people of superior gifts who should aim 'to carry on their lives in their own way'. 'If a person', says Mill, 'possesses any tolerable amount of common sense and experience, his own mode of laying out his existence is the best, not because it is the best in itself, but because it is his own mode'. Human beings are not all alike, and lives, like clothes, need to be individually tailored if they are to fit the individual properly (III. 14). Mill appears to be making at least three claims here: (1) that virtually everyone is capable of choosing a suitable life for him- or herself; (2) that a mode of life that is good for ('fits') one person may not be good for another; and (3) that the life that a person chooses is the best *because* it is the one that he or she has chosen. Each of these propositions is controversial and requires defence, as Mill is aware, though his defences are perhaps not as thoroughgoing as one might wish for.

Mill offers little direct evidence for (1) but defends it obliquely by taking issue with what he describes as the common assumption that people whose lifestyles depart from the norm must be mentally deficient and a consequent danger to themselves. Only those who are high up the social ladder, Mill thinks, can 'indulge somewhat in the luxury of doing as they like' without attracting adverse comment. And even they cannot take things too far: 'for whoever allow themselves much of that indulgence, incur the risk of something worse than disparaging speeches – they are in peril of a commission *de lunatico* [i.e. of being officially declared insane], and of having their property taken from them and given to their relations' (III. 14). In an angry footnote, Mill criticizes the vulgarity and ignorance of the judges, jurors and witnesses in some of the court hearings held to determine the fitness of individuals to manage their affairs. So far from valuing individuality, or the right of people to consult their own judgement and inclination when planning their lives, these courts 'cannot even conceive that a person in a state of sanity can desire such freedom' (III. 14, n.1). In Mill's view, it is nothing but a groundless prejudice to treat the making of unusual choices as evidence of mental incompetence. The default assumption should always be that people know better than others do what is good for them, since only they know their desires and impulses at first hand.

The defence of (2) is grounded on the empirical observation that people differ widely in their personalities, abilities, tastes and desires – or, in Mill's words, 'in their sources of pleasure, their suscept-ibilities of pain, and the operation on them of different physical and moral agencies' (III. 14). When it comes to lives, one size does not fit all:

> [D]ifferent persons ... require different conditions for their spiritual development; and can no more exist healthily in the same moral, than all the variety of plants can in the same phy-sical, atmosphere and climate. The same things which are helps to one person towards the cultivation of his higher nature are hindrances to another. The same mode of life is a healthy excitement to one, keeping all his faculties of action and enjoy-ment in their best order, while to another it is a distracting burthen, which suspends or crushes all internal life. (III. 14)

Given these differences among people, there needs to be 'a corre-sponding diversity in their modes of life'. Otherwise, many persons will 'neither obtain their fair share of happiness, nor grow up to the mental, moral and aesthetic stature of which their nature is capable' (III. 14). This stultification of personal growth and the hindrance of happiness count as major evils on Mill's sophisticated version of utilitarian ethics.

Proposition (3) – that the life that a person has chosen is the best because he or she has chosen it – is probably the most controversial of Mill's three claims. The potential objection to it is that it places too much weight on the fact that a person has chosen his plan of life for himself, and too little on whether that choice is a prudent or sensible one. As Sir Isaiah Berlin has noted, Mill sees man as dif-fering from the animals 'as a being capable of choice, one who is most himself in choosing and not being chosen for'.[14] But there is a distinction between being able to choose and being able to choose well. Mill remarks, rather ambiguously, that a person's choice of a form of life may not always be 'the best in itself'. This might mean that people are sometimes mistaken about their own interests or the best means of promoting them, or that whilst they always choose what is best for themselves, there may be some objectively finer form of life that is not suitable for *them*. But he leaves us in no doubt of his conviction that, in the final analysis, a person's choice will be optimal for him simply because it is his choice. It is not the content of the choice but the fact that the subject has exercised his autonomy in making it that provides most of its value. But are there then, in Mill's view, no limits to admirable eccentricity, and must even the most *outré* of life-choices not only be tolerated (which, for Mill, goes without saying) but regarded as optimal for their subjects?

What should we make, for instance, of a person who devotes her entire life to counting blades of grass, or to ceaselessly repeating the words 'I am a great poet'? We might be inclined to think such choices of lifestyle defective because they have so little connection with the normal economy of a human life. Persons who choose to spend their lives on such apparently aimless activities might reasonably be accused of wasting their time. But could Mill make this accusation, or would he have to grant that their choices, strange though they are, are immune to external criticism?

However, as a careful reading of the text reveals, Mill does *not* say that any life-choices a person may care to make are for her the best possible just because they are hers. He qualifies the boldness of this claim by saying that it applies only to people who possess 'a tolerable amount of common sense and experience'. Although this formulation is vague (exactly how much common sense and experience constitutes 'a tolerable amount'?), it leaves him an opening to say that people like the grass-blade counter or the repetitive poet, in whom common sense is unapparent, have chosen poorly. In justification, Mill might plausibly maintain that a certain measure of rationality can be expected to inform choices that are genuinely autonomous, and that crazy or utterly pointless choices cast doubt on the subject's status as a reasonable self-determining being.

The default assumption that people generally know better than others what is good for them could be cited as further support for proposition (3). And Mill might have added that, even where our choices lack wisdom or prudence, we often learn more from making our own mistakes than we do from following the well-intended advice of other people. Leaving people free to make their own life-choices conduces, besides, to creating that variety of forms of living that makes the world a richer and more interesting place. A form of life that is not cast in one of the ordinary moulds is an experiment in living, a new and valuable exploration of human possibilities.

But what of a person who freely chooses to live a conventional lifestyle? This, too, can represent a fully autonomous choice, and merit respect as such, provided that the lifestyle is selected for its own sake, and not *because* it is conventional. In an incisive discussion of Mill's views on individuality and their implications, Kwame Anthony Appiah argues that it is a mistake to expect that every autonomous choice of a life, every deliberate assumption of an identity, will issue in the unorthodox or unconventional. It may even result, on occasions, in the kind of person who likes to take orders. Appiah illustrates this possibility by the example of Mr Stevens, the efficient and unswervingly loyal butler in Kazuo Ishiguro's novel of inter-war Britain, *The Remains of the Day*. Mr Stevens is a man who has freely chosen to be a butler, and who aspires to be a butler of the very finest kind, dignified yet self-effacing, intelligent and perceptive while eschewing any independence of thought. In effect, he serves two masters: his employer, Lord Darlington, and a certain professional ideal with its constituent virtues. Seeing himself as a butler first and last, Mr Stevens resists any emotional entanglements that might give his life another centre or distract him from the proper performance of his role. Ishiguro represents him as frigid, aloof and introverted, a figure who draws from us feelings at once of pity and respect. Appiah notes that 'Mr Stevens *believes* in decorum, good manners, formality. These compose the world that he has chosen to inhabit and make it the world that it is. ... these may not be values for us, but they *are* values for him, given his plan of life.'[15]

Appiah praises Mill in *On Liberty* for recognizing the important truth that 'sometimes a thing matters because a person has chosen to make a life in which it matters, and that it would not matter if he or she had not chosen to make such a life'.[16] At the same time, cases like that of Mr Stevens are sufficiently disconcerting to make us wonder whether Mill's proposition (3) is not an oversimplification of moral reality. Mr Stevens' decision to live the life of the ideal servitor does not overstep the limits of what a rational human being might choose; it is a far cry from that of the person who devotes an existence to counting blades of grass. But does his choice of that life really make it the best life for him, as (3) implies? We might find it hard to believe that the butler's cherished values merit the exalted regard in which he holds them, or the priority he accords them over other values. Mr Stevens rejects love and marriage in order to devote himself single-mindedly to the cultivation of his professional virtues. Had he decided differently and married the woman he loves, that too, according to (3) would have been the best choice for him. But we might think that it would also have been a better choice on account of the fuller and happier life it would have brought him. John Gray suggests that choosing a more ordinary in preference to a more distinctive course of life is sometimes better for a person's well-being.[17] A married Mr Stevens might have been a less distinctive individual but a more contented man.

However, in passing this judgement, we help ourselves to an assumption that Mill and Appiah might well challenge: namely, the assumption that it would have been the *same* Mr Stevens who would have been happier had he made that choice. But since the actual Mr Stevens is the man who chose the butler's life, it is unclear that *that* man would have been better off in the married state; for all we know, the decision to marry might have turned out to be tragically wrong for him, leading to an unbearable inner struggle between conflicting values. That a different Mr Stevens (one with warmer emotions or less focused on the servitor's role) might have married happily does not show that the actual Mr Stevens could have done so. Marriage might *not* have enhanced the real Mr Stevens' well-being. Hence the intuitive reservations we may feel about proposition (3) may be harder to sustain than they first seemed. Where our perspective on values differs from the perspective of those whose life-choices we attempt to judge, *our* judgements will seem irrelevant and misguided to *them*, just as theirs will to us. Perhaps the most we can say in such cases is that *we* would not have made the choices they have done; but the fact that their choices would have been wrong for us does not entail that they were wrong for them.

III. 15–19: The praise of pluralism (2): The 'despotism of custom'

Mill wryly observes in paragraph 15 that most people are so conventional in their own inclinations that they scornfully dismiss as 'wild and intemperate' anyone who is disposed to do anything in the least out of the ordinary. To make matters worse, there has lately set in a movement for the improvement of morals which threatens to produce even more 'regularity of conduct and discouragement of excesses'. The aim of this movement is to make everyone conform to an approved standard of conduct whose central tenet is that one should desire nothing strongly. In Mill's withering description:

> Its ideal of character is to be without any marked character; to maim by compression, like a Chinese lady's foot, every part of human nature which stands out prominently, and tends to make the person markedly dissimilar in outline to commonplace humanity. (III. 15)

What Berlin terms 'Mill's overmastering desire for variety and individuality for their own sake' dominates the closing pages of chapter III.[18] Mill laments the disappearance of 'energetic characters on any large scale', scornfully adding that '[t]here is now scarcely any outlet of energy in this country except business' (III. 16). The result of the prevailing standard of conduct is that '[i]nstead of great energies guided by vigorous reason, and strong feelings controlled by a conscientious will', there are only 'weak feelings and weak energies, which therefore can be kept in outward conformity to rule without any strength either of will or reason'. It was men of a different stamp that made England what it is, and who will be needed if it is not to decline (III. 16).

According to Mill, the 'despotism of custom' is 'the standing hindrance to human advancement'. It is 'in unceasing antagonism to that disposition to aim at something better than customary, which is called ... the spirit of liberty, or that of progress or improvement' (III. 17). Most of the world is already under its sway, because people have abandoned individuality and originality as ideals. Worse, there are well-meaning and deeply misguided people who are doing their best to banish them. Mill speaks rather mysteriously of 'English philanthropists' who are 'industriously working' at 'making a people all alike, all governing their thoughts and conduct by the same maxims and rules' (III. 17). It is not clear whether Mill is referring to any specific figures here or whether he is thinking more generally of all those who are backing the 'improvement of morals' mentioned in paragraph 15. In a further echo of de Tocqueville, Mill locates the chief source of danger in the power of public opinion. If individuality is going to survive, he warns, it must vigorously defend itself:

The modern *regime* of public opinion is, in an unorganised form, what the Chinese educational and political systems are in an organised; and unless individuality shall be able successfully to assert itself against this yoke, Europe, notwithstanding its noble antecedent and its professed Christianity, will tend to become another China. (III. 17)

What has preserved Europe from this fate so far? In Mill's view, only its 'remarkable diversity of character and culture'. Europeans have 'struck out on a great variety of paths, each leading to something valuable', and while they have not always shown much tolerance for one another's efforts, their attempts to compel others to travel their own roads have mostly failed. Almost in spite of themselves, Europeans have learned valuable lessons from other people's different ways of doing things. 'Europe is, in my judgement', Mill concludes, 'wholly indebted to this plurality of paths for its progressive and many-sided development' (III. 18).

Human development requires not only individual freedom but also what Mill calls 'variety of situations'. Yet such variety is in the process of disappearing as 'different ranks, different neighbourhoods, different trades and professions', who once occupied separate worlds, come to share the same one. Mill attributes this change to the decline in the distances between the social classes, the notable developments in education and communications, and the increase in personal opportunities for social and economic advancement. Mill does not regret these changes, which he recognizes have improved life for many. His claim is not that they are bad, but that they are not unalloyed goods, since they bring with them a danger of conformity – a 'general similarity of mankind' – which is the more insidious because its advent is gradual and easily overlooked. The 'complete ascendancy of public opinion' which will result from them will, unless it is countered, drive the final nail into the coffin of individuality (III. 18).

Already, Mill thinks, it is hard to see how individuality can stand its ground. But all hope is not lost provided that 'the intelligent part of the public can be made to see its value – to see that it is good there should be differences, even though not for the better, even though, as it may appear to them, some should be for the worse'. This plain statement of a pluralist position is Mill's final rallying-cry in the chapter to all who care about individuality to come to its defence. If they delay, then the very concept of individuality will be lost, for '[m]ankind speedily become unable to conceive diversity, when they have been for some time unaccustomed to see it' (III. 19).

We have questioned whether Mill was justified in supposing that individuality in Victorian Britain was in its last gasp. But if he was too pessimistic on that score, he may have been over-optimistic on another. Mill assumes that, freed from the force of custom, people will react like coiled springs that are suddenly released, revealing an energy and individuality of which they had previously shown no sign. This may be little more than wishful thinking. A lot of people might simply be lost without custom to guide them. Many, too, may have little inclination or ability to develop themselves in new and original ways, or to conduct 'experiments of living' of the kind Mill called for. Some might opt to live safe, staid or unadventurous lives which involve no very energetic development of their talents. Mill's intense respect for individual autonomy would make it difficult for him to criticise people who make a reflective choice to pursue the cautious rather than the daring course, or who have less exalted ideals of self-development than he does. An implication of promoting pluralism is that one has to be ready to put up with styles of life that one may find uncongenial, disappointing or distasteful. Mill would not, of course, wish to see those who waste their talents, or whose lives contain unfulfilled potential, compelled to mend their ways. But his confidence that humanity only needs to be freed from the constraints of custom to produce a wonderful flowering of creative activity may be more romantic than realistic. Perhaps those with genuine native genius would benefit from the absence of moulds and templates into which all creative production had to be fitted. Yet energetic and talented individuals are not so easily repressed in any age, one of the marks of genius being that it tends to find an outlet however unfavourable the social circumstances.

It is interesting to contrast Mill's despondent view of individuality at the mid-century with the much more upbeat assessment of the great Whig statesman and sometime prime minister Lord Palmerston. Speaking at a prize-giving ceremony at the South London Industrial Exhibition in 1865, Palmerston praised 'the happy influences of the constitution under which we have the good fortune to live', which 'opens up to every man having talents, energy, perseverance, and good conduct any honours and distinctions which his turn of mind and attainments may qualify him to aspire to'. Many men from the humblest beginnings, he observed, had risen to the highest places in business, politics and the professions.[19] Whether what Palmerston saw as 'removable inequalities' were quite so easy to remove as he claimed they were has been doubted by some historians; and modern readers will notice the absence from his speech of any reference to the opportunities open to women. But Palmerston's high regard for individual endeavour mirrors Mill's, as does his reference, in an earlier speech of 1850, to the characteristic display, by the average British citizen, of 'persevering good conduct, and ... the steady and energetic exertion of the moral and intellectual faculties with which his creator has endowed him'.[20] That Palmerston, the aristocratic grandee, and Mill, the trenchant liberal critic of contemporary mores, could praise the same qualities and in similar terms indicates that the ideals defended in *On Liberty* were more commonly upheld, and less endangered, than Mill allowed.

It is also possible to question Mill's unqualified condemnation of custom and convention as being altogether bad. If the customs and traditions of a society may be felt by its members as frustrating and confining, they can also be experienced as supportive and empowering. Socially accepted practices, tried and tested and yielding predictable results, are often more reliable means of realizing good ends than novel individual experiments. Adhering to the same rules and standards as others can also strengthen social bonds, enhancing the sense of fraternity and common purpose. A society that lacked traditions and customs would hardly be recognizable as a society. It is therefore not clear that there could be a *society* of pure Millian individualists. Unsympathetically considered, Mill's advice that we should continually strive to be original and unconventional sounds like a recipe for social alienation. It would be hard to feel much kinship with our neighbours if we were constantly seeking to be different from them. Many philosophers from Aristotle onwards have thought that human beings live best when they cultivate their interpersonal relationships in a context of shared values and goals. John Donne famously declared that no man is an island. However, a 'society' of individualists would resemble less a community of like-minded and like-feeling persons than an archipelago of islands.

Mill's optimism about the use which people would make of increased freedom from custom was severely criticized by one of his most hostile readers, James Fitzjames Stephen. Stephen thought it extremely unlikely that most people would find in such freedom an opportunity for self-development. Mill, he complained, held 'too favourable' a view of what human nature would produce when not subject to controls. In contrast, Stephen thought that '[h]abitual exertion is the greatest of all invigorators of character, and restraint and coercion in one form or another is the great stimulus to exertion'. Most persons if left to themselves would choose comfort and ease in preference to energetic activity; therefore they must not be left to themselves. Stephen granted that many people have the potential to achieve worthwhile things but he disagreed profoundly with Mill on how best to bring this out. In his view, creative activity is not effectively promoted via Millian liberty, since '[a]lmost every human being requires more or less coercion and restraint as astringents to give him the maximum of power which he is capable of attaining'.[21]

If Mill exhibits at times an over-romantic view of human nature, Stephen presents us with a far darker portrait. 'Speak of original sin or not as you please', he wrote, 'but the fact that all men are in some respects and at some times both weak and wicked, that they do the ill they would not do, and shun the good they would pursue, is no less certain'.[22] Even the best people are only indifferently honest, and need keeping up to the mark. Those who are not so good require considerably more help to stay on the straight and narrow. Encouraging people to be different, Stephen argued, is effectively encouraging licence – a point that Mill failed to recognize because he naively supposed that human beings would use their freedom to develop their strengths rather than indulge their weaknesses. Stephen thought that Mill was simply wrong about this. On his own less sanguine outlook, encouraging variety for the sake of it is foolish and irresponsible. To be different is not necessarily to be better. In a shrewd hit, Stephen remarked that if Mill's advice to 'dare to be eccentric' were generally followed, 'we should have as many little oddities in manner and behaviour as we have people who wish to pass for men of genius'.[23] While it is right to value originality, Mill was too apt to forget that '[o]riginality consists in thinking for yourself, not in thinking differently from other people'.[24]

Defending Mill against Stephen's attack, Mill's friend and disciple John Morley argued that the latter had misunderstood the doctrine of individuality offered in *On Liberty*. Mill had never, claimed Morley, praised variety for its own sake. Mill thought variety to be important for the much more solid reason that 'it furnishes most chances of new forms of good presenting themselves and acquiring a permanent place'. Unless people are prepared to depart from custom, there can be little prospect of 'new ideas, new practices, new sentiments' – and hence of 'future improvements in the arts of existence'.[25] But Stephen was unimpressed by Morley's response. Although he admitted that variety sometimes has the beneficial consequences that Mill and Morley claimed for it, he persisted in thinking their praise of variety overdone. Many instances of variety were trivial, or worse, while many examples of custom were sound and beneficial and had stood the test of time.[26]

Does Mill or Stephen ultimately have the better of the argument? This is something that readers need to decide for themselves. It may be that the truth lies somewhere in between and that neither variety nor conformity should be considered altogether good or altogether bad. Perhaps the best social arrangements allow for a judicious mixture of both. There is no necessary opposition between encouraging individuality and fostering people's sense of their social identity by upholding some traditions and conventions. (It might also be argued that mid-Victorian Britain achieved a fairly close approximation to this happy state of affairs).

Yet if neither Mill nor Stephen gets the balance exactly right, it is hard not to find Mill's message a more inspiring one than Stephen's. Mill's vision, like Aristotle's, focuses on the moral and intellectual excellences of which human beings are capable; Stephen's view concentrates instead on human faults and weaknesses. If for Aristotle and Mill, humanity has a spark of the divine about it, for Stephen all members of the species have feet of clay. Stephen's more sombre perspective may offer a useful corrective to Mill's tendency to expect too much of human beings in a state of liberty; yet Mill sets before us more attractive ideals to guide our aspirations. In the last analysis, the dispute between Mill and Stephen may offer a good illustration of Mill's own claim, in chapter II, that often 'conflicting doctrines, instead of being one true and the other false, share the truth between them' (II. 34).

Study Questions

1. Is individuality always a good thing?
2. Is custom always a bad thing?
3. How persuasive is Mill that freedom is a necessary condition for the development of all that is best in human beings?
4. Should we conduct 'experiments of living'? What benefits might these provide, and what dangers may be associated with them?
5. Are people always the best judges of their own well-being?
6. Was Mill justified in believing the 'despotism of custom' to be a significant danger in the mid-Victorian period?

CHAPTER IV: OF THE LIMITS TO THE AUTHORITY OF SOCIETY OVER THE INDIVIDUAL

IV. 1–3: Social and individual spheres distinguished

Chapter IV of *On Liberty* may be thought of as an extended disquisition on the harm principle introduced in chapter I. Mill's 'one very simple principle', we may recall, is that 'self-protection' is the only basis on which interference with individual liberty can be tolerated: 'the only purpose for which power can be rightfully exercised over a member of a civilised community, is to prevent harm to others' (I. 9). The simplicity of the principle consists in its specifying a single criterion by which restrictions of liberty can be justified. But, as Mill is well aware, providing a precise interpretation of that criterion and clarifying the conditions of its application are matters calling for some finesse. It is to these tasks he turns in chapter IV. Bain, after noting that the chapter 'helps us better to [Mill's] real meaning', praised it as an admirable exposition in practical ethics which 'might be enshrined as a standing homily in the moral instruction of mankind'.[1] Subsequent readers, while not always accepting Mill's conclusions, have agreed with Bain's assessment of it as a seminal text on the limits of individual liberty.

Mill sets out the leading questions of the chapter in a terse first paragraph: 'What, then, is the rightful limit to the sovereignty of the individual over himself? Where does the authority of society begin? How much of human life should be assigned to individuality, and how much to society?' (IV. I). His outline response to these questions is that to individuality belongs 'the part of life in which it is chiefly the individual that is interested', and to society 'the part which chiefly interests society' (IV. 2). But he is well aware that these answers are not very helpful unless the boundary between the social and the individual 'parts of life' can be settled with more exactness. Mill rejects the idea (maintained, for instance, by Thomas Hobbes in *Leviathan* [1651]) that civil society is founded on a contract between its constituent members. Nevertheless, he accepts that social living imposes obligations on individuals: 'every one who receives the protection of society owes a return for the benefit, and the fact of living in society renders it indispensable that each should be bound to observe a certain line of conduct towards the rest' (IV. 3). To live peaceably and happily with others, we must be prepared to give as well as take. So we must be willing to bear our share of 'the labours and sacrifices incurred for defending the society or its members from injury and molestation'. And we must obviously cause no harm to our fellow-citizens. If we fall short in meeting these responsibilities, we may render ourselves liable to sanctions. Mill draws an interesting distinction between acts which violate others' 'constituted [i.e. legally protected] rights', for which we may suffer judicial punishment, and those which, while hurtful or inconsiderate, do not; in the case of the latter, we 'may be justly punished by opinion, though not by law' (IV. 3). (So if, for example, I always push my way to the head of any queue I wish to join, I may not be infringing anyone's legal rights but my selfish behaviour will be condemned and may redound to my cost if ever I seek the help of others).

Mill sets out the general principle governing legitimate interference with some care:

> As soon as any part of a person's conduct affects prejudicially the interests of others, society has jurisdiction over it, and the question whether the general welfare will or will not be promoted by interfering with it, becomes open to discussion. But there is no room for entertaining any such question when a person's conduct affects the interests of no persons besides himself, or needs not affect them unless they like (all the persons concerned being of full age, and the ordinary amount of understanding). In all such cases, there should be perfect freedom, legal and social, to do the action and stand the consequences. (IV. 3)

This is essentially the harm principle, more elaborately stated and with the important gloss added that where a person's actions affect the interests of other adult people of normal intelligence, it is up to them, rather than society, to give or refuse consent to them. If I propose to do something that is actually or potentially damaging to your well-being, it is your right, and no one else's, to decide whether I may go ahead. If you are willing to sacrifice your interests to mine, then well and good; but I may not proceed without your permission, nor may any third party give or refuse consent on your behalf.

IV. 4–7: Compulsion, persuasion and the self-regarding virtues

But might this not be read as a doctrine of selfish indifference, according to which we should concern ourselves narrowly with our own good and pay no attention to whether others are living or doing well? (One might also ask, though Mill does not, whether such a doctrine is compatible with utilitarianism, which enjoins us always to act so as to maximise human well-being). Mill responds to this question in paragraph 4, where he firmly rebuts the notion that other people's welfare concerns us only in so far as we have a duty not to harm them. We *should* take an active interest in promoting other people's well-being, and in helping them to promote their own; but there are right and wrong ways to do this. Mill stresses that while 'there is need of a great increase of disinterested exertion to promote the good of others ... disinterested benevolence can find other instruments to persuade people to their good than whips and scourges, either of the literal or the metaphorical sort'. We should work by persuasion, rather than compulsion; and we should dismiss the illusion that people can be forced to be virtuous (IV. 4).

Mill thinks it crucial to their well-being that people should possess 'the self-regarding virtues'. In lieu of a crisp definition of self-regarding virtue, he writes that people 'should be for ever stimulating each other to increased exercise of their higher faculties, and increased direction of their feelings and aims towards wise instead of foolish, elevating instead of degrading, objects and contemplations' (IV. 4). Self-regarding virtues thus have to do with personal self-development, and we may suppose that Mill thinks of them both as aiding that development, and as constituting the chief excellence of those who have acquired them.

Inculcating the self-regarding virtues, he suggests, is one of the major roles of childhood education (another is instilling the social virtues, or the habits of caring for others). Although the education of the young will inevitably involve some compulsion, educators should work wherever possible 'by conviction and persuasion'. But once a person is grown up, education of the formal kind must stop. For:

> neither one person, nor any number of persons, is warranted in saying to another human creature of ripe years, that he shall not do with his life for his own benefit what he chooses to do with it. He is the person most interested in his own well-being: the interest which any other person, except in cases of strong personal attachment, can have in it, is trifling, compared with that which he himself has; ... while with respect to his own feelings and circumstances, the most ordinary man or woman has means of knowledge immeasurably surpassing those that can be possessed by any one else. (IV. 4)

'Individuality has its proper field of action' in each person's 'own concerns'. Other people may offer suggestions, or exhortations to strengthen an agent's will, and Mill even proposes that they may 'obtrude' these on his attention, though he is disappointingly unspecific about the point at which forceful persuasion turns into improper compulsion. But they must not 'constrain him to what they deem his good', for he alone must be the final judge of that (IV. 4).

Mill's view that we may advise and admonish when we think these will do people good, but must stop short of seeking to control them, is strikingly reminiscent of Locke's. A person's salvation, Locke held, is entirely his own affair. 'But I would not have this understood', he continues, 'as if I meant hereby to condemn all charitable admonitions, and affectionate endeavours to reduce men from errors, which are indeed the greatest duty of a Christian. Any one may employ as many exhortations and arguments as he pleases, towards the promoting of another man's salvation. But all force and compulsion are to be forborne'[2]. Mill's position is a straight-forward generalization of this, with Locke's principle of persuade-but-do-not-compel exported from the sphere of religious salvation to that of personal well-being more broadly conceived.

People's self-regarding qualities, or their lack of them, will naturally affect how others regard and relate to them. Someone who is 'eminent in any of the qualities which conduce to his own good' will tend to be admired, while one who is greatly deficient in them will become 'a subject of distaste, or, in extreme cases, even of contempt' (IV. 5). Since people who fail to acquire the self-regarding virtues are letting themselves down rather than harming others, it would be wrong to try to make them develop these qualities. But Mill regrets that current standards of politeness do not permit more robust practices of criticism and advice; it would be a good thing, he thinks, 'if one person could honestly point out to another that he thinks him in fault, without being considered unmannerly or presuming' (IV. 5). Although this is little more than an aside, one wonders whether Mill would really welcome a world in which people candidly told one another to their faces what they thought of them. Probably those who would most eagerly assume this Big-Brotherly role are the very 'improvers of morals' whose assistance in imposing the 'despotism of custom' he so strongly deplored in the previous chapter. It is likely, too, that the people who were most in need of criticism or guidance would be the ones least willing to pay any heed to it.

Mill reasonably remarks that we have a right to 'act upon our unfavourable opinion of any one, not to the oppression of his individuality, but in the exercise of ours'. We may choose our own company and are not obliged to mix with people we disapprove of or dislike. Nor can those whom we disfavour justly complain if we give others the preference in 'optional good offices', except those which might lead to their improvement. Someone who is rash, obstinate, conceited, wasteful and who 'cannot restrain himself from hurtful indulgences', cannot expect to be treated on a par with another who is free of these vices (IV. 5). People must be prepared to put up with 'the inconveniences which are strictly inseparable from the unfavourable judgement of others' (IV. 6). It is no one else's business to force them to be better, or to punish them for their self-regarding defects; but others are within their rights to give them a wide berth.

But how exactly do we draw the line between allowing the subjects of self-regarding defects to suffer 'inconveniences', and inflicting punishment on them? Mill is once again not very specific. Imagine that you were an employer choosing between two candidates for a job, both of whom appeared equally able to fulfil its requirements, but one of whom had considerably more self-regarding defects than the other (say, he was arrogant, vain, loud-mouthed and untidy). Would Mill approve of your offering the job to the more likeable candidate? Or would he count this as a punishment which goes beyond the limits of permissible reproof or avoidance? In rejecting the less virtuous candidate you may have no deliberate intention of punishing him; you may simply believe that the other candidate would be the pleasanter colleague to work with. But the fact remains that you have subjected the unsuccessful applicant to significant relative disadvantage on account of his less endearing personal qualities. If this is not meant as a punishment, it may nevertheless be felt as one if the candidate finds out the reason for his rejection.

Bain observes in relation to this passage that Mill might usefully 'have gone further and drawn up a sliding scale or graduated table of modes of behaviour, from the most intense individual preference at the one end to the severest reprobation [accompanied, presumably, by punishment] at the other'. He adds that '[a]t least fifteen or twenty perceptible distinctions could be made, and a place found for every degree of merit or demerit'.[3] Bain is correct that a spectrum of responses to people's self-regarding faults is possible, though his estimate of 'fifteen or twenty' distinguishable points seems arbitrary. But he appears not to notice that the absence of a clear-cut divide between suffering inconvenience and being punished is problematic for Mill. Nor does he seem aware of the ethical difficulty associated with the fact that 'mere' inconveniences which are inseparable from the unfavourable judgement of others can have a harsher subjective impact than some formal punishments.

In paragraph 6, Mill reiterates that it is only *self*-regarding faults that should be immune to punishment or control, and that '[a]cts injurious to others require a totally different treatment'. The latter 'are fit objects of moral reprobation, and, in grave cases, of moral retribution and punishment'. They alone are the true immoralities, Mill adds, since self-regarding faults, even when carried to extremes, are not, properly speaking, wicked. Some readers may be uneasy with this attempt to restrict the term 'immoral' to other-regarding faults and acts, even if they agree that these should not be subject to interference by others. Possibly Mill is motivated by a desire to undercut one popular pretext for punishing self-regarding defects, namely that they are immoral; but since he has other and better grounds for rejecting this position he has no real need to resort to a dubious linguistic stipulation.

Of more serious practical import is Mill's proposal that not only the acts that harm other people 'but the dispositions which lead to them, are properly immoral, and fit subjects of disapprobation which may rise to abhorrence'. The list of such bad dispositions includes cruelty, malice, envy, greed, 'irascibility on insufficient cause', the love of domination, the delight in others' abasement, and 'the egotism which thinks self and its concerns more important than everything else' (IV. 6)

Unfortunately, Mill does not explain at all clearly how we should respond to such bad dispositions, saying only that their owners may be 'held accountable' for them. He would presumably not approve of punishing a person for, say, having a cruel or grasping disposition, as distinct from performing cruel or greedy acts. People can be held morally responsible for what they *do*, but not for the dispositions which nature has given them. It is less apparent whether he would favour forcibly preventing people who had cruel or greedy dispositions from occupying positions of influence or authority which might offer tempting opportunities to indulge them. It would be hard to organize a fair and efficient system for monitoring personal dispositions, and the level of intrusion into private lives that it would require would be deeply troubling for Mill. (There would also arise the difficult question, as with any structure in which one set of people exercises power over another, of who would then 'guard the guardians'). But Mill might be willing to see the operation of such arrangements in some limited circumstances, perhaps where individuals had already shown signs of a willingness to act on their harmful dispositions. He might well have approved, for instance, of the current regulations in the UK which forbid persons on the Sex-Offenders Register being employed in any capacity which brings them into close contact with children, e.g. as teachers, school caretakers or youth leaders. Where constraints of this kind are, for practical or ethical reasons, undesirable, Mill would probably wish us to offer moral encouragement and advice instead – just as we should do in regard to people's self-regarding defects.

Once a person has acted on his bad disposition and 'infringed the rules necessary for the protection of his fellow-creatures', Mill is adamant that he must then be punished. Since he has caused harm to others, 'society, as the protector of all its members, must retaliate on him; must inflict pain on him for the express purpose of punishment, and must take care that it be sufficiently severe' (IV. 7). Anger and resentment are now in order, unlike when a person damages himself alone through his self-regarding defects. Mill's use of words such as 'retaliate' and 'resentment' is strongly suggestive of a *retributivist* view of punishment, which holds that society has a right and a duty to ensure that offenders against the social order receive their 'just deserts'. Retributivist accounts of punishment are usually contrasted with utilitarian or *deterrentist* ones, which locate the primary warrant for punishment in its capacity to deter people from committing similar offences in future. Retributivism can be thought of as a backward-looking theory, which sees punishment as serving to restore the moral balance that has been disturbed by an offence; deterrentism, by contrast, looks forward to the beneficial consequences (a reduction in the number or seriousness of offences) of inflicting punishment.

It may be thought curious that Mill, as a confirmed utilitarian, sounds more retributivist than deterrentist in paragraph 7. But in *On Liberty* he is not really interested in defending any particular theory of punishment. His aim is rather to draw attention to the different attitudes we may properly hold towards people on account of their self-regarding and their other-regarding faults. The person with self-regarding defects 'may be to us an object of pity, perhaps of dislike, but not of anger or resentment' – the latter attitudes are appropriate *only* in regard to the harm that agents do, or are disposed to do, to others. People have no business to feel angry or resentful about things which are an individual's private concern. We may note in passing, however, that Mill, unlike some other writers on punishment, saw no essential incompatibility between the notions of retribution and deterrence. The celebrated speech he delivered to the House of Commons in 1868 in favour of retaining the death penalty contains elements of both retributivist and deterrentist thinking.[4] While Mill, like other utilitarians, thought that punishment should achieve some useful practical result, he also saw it as a medium for discharging the justified emotions of anger and indignation that offences done to others arouse.

IV. 8–13: The case against controlling people in their own interests

The arguments that Mill has so far deployed against attempts by 'society, individually or collectively' to control or constrain individuals in their own interests may, though, be thought to rest on an objectionable assumption, namely that a sharp distinction can be drawn between 'the part of a person's life which concerns only himself, and that which concerns others' (IV. 8). Given the inter-connectedness of the lives of those who share a common social environment, this assumption, as Mill recognizes, is contestable:

> How (it may be asked) can any part of the conduct of a member of society be a matter of indifference to the other members? No person is an entirely isolated being; it is impossible for a person to do anything seriously or permanently hurtful to himself, without mischief reaching at least to his near connections, and often far beyond them. (IV. 8)

Mill breaks down the kind of damage that a self-harming person may also be causing to others into three categories. First, if he injures his property, he does harm to any besides himself who benefit from it, while in some cases he may diminish the resources of the whole community. Second, if he wastes or abuses his physical or mental faculties, he lets down those who rely on his keeping himself in good shape (e.g. his family, friends or colleagues) and becomes a less useful member of society; he may also, in the worst cases, come to depend on society for his own support. Third, even if his vices and follies cause no direct harm to others, he may be doing harm more subtly by the bad example that he sets (IV. 8).

Apart from the self-interested reasons that society may have for interfering in the lives of those who damage others in these ways, it could also be accused of failing in charity to its own weaker members if it did nothing to rescue them from the sour fruits of their own stupidity or fecklessness. Arguably society should not 'abandon to their own guidance those who are manifestly unfit for it'. If children and young people are regularly protected against themselves, why should the same not happen in the case of those adults 'who are equally incapable of self-government'? (IV. 9). Mill notes that two different modes of control might suggest themselves for dealing with people who surrender themselves to 'gambling, or drunkenness, or incontinence [i.e. lack of self-control], or idle-ness, or uncleanliness [the euphemistic Victorian term for sexual promiscuity]'. First, laws could be introduced to repress these hindrances to happiness and 'improvement'. Second, as a supplementary measure, public opinion could be brought into play and 'organise a powerful police against these vices, and visit rigidly with social penalties those who are known to practise them'. To avoid the objection that such methods of control would restrict individuality and impede new experiments in living, care could be taken to prevent nothing except 'things which have been tried and condemned from the beginning of the world until now; things which experience has shown not to be useful or suitable to any person's individuality' (IV. 9).

Against these exceedingly illiberal proposals, Mill offers three powerful counter-arguments, in paragraphs 10 through 12.

Counter-argument 1 (IV. 10). Mill readily admits that when people harm themselves, they may also do considerable damage to others, both those who are closely connected to them through their interests and sympathies and the members of the community at large. But wherever this is so, 'the case is taken out of the self-regarding class, and becomes amenable to moral disapprobation in the proper sense of the term' – in other words, it is morally objectionable because it infringes the harm principle. Mill provides examples to make this important point plain:

> If ... a man, through intemperance or extravagance, becomes unable to pay his debts, or, having undertaken the moral responsibility of a family, becomes from the same cause incapable of supporting or educating them, he is deservedly reprobated, and might be justly punished; *but it is for the breach of duty to his family or creditors, not for the extravagance.* (IV. 10; emphasis added)

A person may damage himself by his bad habits, but in so far as his errors are 'merely personal to himself' they remain his own business. However, the moment that his weakness, folly or fecklessness start to impact negatively on others, they become society's business; a private matter has become a public concern. 'In like manner', Mill continues, 'when a person disables himself, by conduct purely self-regarding, from the performance of some definite duty incumbent on him to the public, he is guilty of a social offence'. So while no one should be punished just for getting drunk, it would be reasonable to punish a soldier or a policeman for being drunk while on duty.

Mill is surely right to point out that the causal interconnectedness of lives is not in itself a sufficient basis for permitting social interference with individual choices, so long as we can distinguish between the harm that people's choices do to themselves and the harm they do to others. There will, however, be borderline cases where it is debatable whether the amount of harm that a self-regarding choice causes to other people is sufficient to warrant any external intervention. Ought anything to be done about the gambler or heavy drinker who 'blows' a large proportion of the household income on his vice, but who is conscientious enough to ensure that his family have just enough money to live on? Should society intervene in the case of a person whose ability to discharge her family or professional responsibilities is impaired but not wholly undermined by her alcoholism or drug-taking? Mill would, of course, recommend exhorting such people to mend their ways. But at what stage does something more forceful than mere exhortation become appropriate? Mill remarks of the man who 'causes grief to his family by his addiction to bad habits' that he 'deserves reproach for his unkindness or ingratitude' (IV. 10). But he does not tell us where the line between 'grief' and injury lies, or what should be done in those cases that lie on or near to it.

Mill's acknowledgement that people's 'self-regarding' choices can have a profound effect on others may make us wonder whether the label 'self-regarding' is really apposite on such occasions. If a husband's addiction to drink or gambling causes grief or injury to his wife and family, then it would appear to include a considerable other-regarding along with its self-regarding element. Mill would probably defend his terminology by reference to the causal sequence involved: the drunkard who allows his dependants to sink into a state of poverty harms them, but he does so via the harmful choice he has already made for himself. Unlike the cruel or sadistic man who beats his children for the sheer fun of it, the drunkard's primary problem is a self-regarding weakness rather than an other-regarding vice. Yet human moral psychology is rarely simple and it is likely that in many cases of moral dereliction a more complex story can be told. Thus a man who drinks away the household income may be flawed not just by a self-regarding weakness for drink but also by the other-regarding defect of a cold and unsympathetic nature, grounded (perhaps) in an inability to empathise with others.

Counter-argument 2 (IV. 11). Mill's second argument is directed against the claim that people may be punished when, through not taking proper care of themselves, they impair their ability to contribute positively to the social good. It would be wrong, he asserts, to punish individuals for not adding to the general good in ways 'which society does not pretend it has a right to exact'. Such contributions have a quite different moral status to those which a person is duty-bound to make. An alcoholic writer whose family goes hungry as a result of his non-production fails in his duty to look after them properly, and lays himself open to penalties. But he should not be further punished for failing to write the fine books he could have produced. Society, or the reading portion of it, does not have the right to require him to keep up a steady output of good books. Although it loses out as a result of his drinking, this is the kind of inconvenience which Mill thinks 'society can afford to bear, for the sake of the greater good of human freedom'.

To bolster the second counter-argument, Mill reminds us that society has its chance to mould its members into useful citizens while they are still children. This is the time for bringing any 'weaker members' up to society's 'ordinary standard of rational conduct':

Society has absolute power over them during all the early portion of their existence: it has had the whole period of childhood and nonage [i.e. youth] in which to try whether it could make them capable of rational conduct in life. ... If society lets any considerable number of its members grow up mere children, incapable of being acted on by rational consideration of distant motives, society has itself to blame for the consequences. (IV. 11)

Attempting to coerce adult persons into being more prudent or temperate is, in any case, liable to be self-defeating, producing resentment rather than improvement. Any 'vigorous and independent characters' will 'infallibly rebel against the yoke' and do the opposite of what is demanded of them.

But what about the worry that those who indulge their self-regarding weaknesses pose a danger of corrupting the innocent by their bad example? Mill rejects this as a reason for using coercive tactics on the ground that, since these people provide an example of *self-harm*, this should 'be more salutary than hurtful', showing the 'painful or degrading consequences' of the conduct at issue (IV. 11). This response may owe more to hope than to experience. Gertrude Himmelfarb comments that Mill appears to accept 'a providential view of human conduct, in which immorality redounds immediately, directly, and manifestly to the disadvantage of the perpetrator himself'. Whilst Mill may not have believed 'in an avenging God, he seems to have believed, at least "on the whole", in an avenging moral order'.[5] Such a view, she implies, is naive. Some immoral people never have to pay a price – or what they would regard as one – for their bad behaviour. They live what are, by their standards, satisfactory lives, which they see no reason to alter. Mill may also be forgetting what religious writers have called 'the glamour of evil' – the apparent, if specious, attractiveness that bad things can possess, sometimes precisely because they are frowned on by the virtuous. Those who take risks with their own health or well-being may also be seen as models of spurious ideals of daring, insouciance or unconventionality. Given Mill's own fascination with eccentricity and his advocacy of 'experiments in living', he is surprisingly complacent about the potential danger afforded by inappropriate role models, especially to the young and inexperienced. Since he considers their moral education a social responsibility, he could consistently, if reluctantly, have invoked the harm principle to justify the coercion of individuals who set a bad example.

Counter-argument 3 (IV. 12). Mill reserves until last what he takes to be the strongest argument against the interference of the public with 'purely personal conduct'. When society does interfere, he contends, 'the odds are that it interferes wrongly, and in the wrong place'. Mill distinguishes between society's judgements of its own interests and its judgements of the interests of individuals, and he suggests that the former are a lot more reliable than the latter. The claim that the public is good at judging 'questions of social morality, of duty to others' and of estimating the effects on itself of a particular type of conduct may sound odd coming from someone who believes that contemporary society is imprudently submitting to be governed by the 'despotism of custom'. But Mill is on firmer ground in rebutting the idea that society knows best what is good for individuals:

> the opinion of a ... majority, imposed by law on a minority, on questions of self-regarding conduct, is quite as likely to be wrong as right; for in these cases public opinion means, at the best, some people's opinion of what is good or bad for other people;

while very often it does not even mean that; the public, with the most perfect indifference, passing over the pleasure or convenience of those whose conduct they censure, and considering only their own preference. (IV. 12)

Mill proceeds, with some subtlety, to locate the heart of the problem. There are many people, he notes, 'who consider as an injury to themselves any conduct which they have a distaste for'. Religious bigots, for example, frequently complain that others are disregarding *their* feelings when they follow their abominable creed. In response, Mill states a highly important principle:

[T]here is no parity between the feeling of a person for his own opinion, and the feeling of another who is offended at his holding it; no more than between the desire of a thief to take a purse, and the desire of the right owner to keep it. (IV. 12)

People's actions, opinions and tastes in relation to self-regarding matters are strictly their own concern, and no one else has a right to dictate what they should be, anymore than they have a right to spend their money for them. A person is under no obligation to suppress or moderate a particular like or dislike just because others – even if there are a lot of others – dislike his holding it. Such second-order likes and dislikes (i.e. likes and dislikes which have other likes or dislikes as their objects) are not to be weighed in the same scale with their first-order counterparts. If Smith, an aficionado of palm-court orchestras, is pained by Jones's liking for the most strident kind of jungle music, Smith's second-order attitude provides, on Mill's thinking, no reason whatever for Jones to try to alter his taste. Smith and Jones should simply agree to differ, and adopt a mutual stance of 'Live, and let live'.

But why are people so often reluctant to do this, especially in regard to moral matters? Because, Mill suggests, they wrongly see their own opinions and principles as setting the standard by which all others should be judged. When the public tries to interfere with individual conduct, 'it is seldom thinking of anything but the enormity of acting or feeling differently from itself'. To make matters worse, 'this standard of judgement, thinly disguised, is held up to mankind as the dictate of religion and philosophy, by nine-tenths of all moralists and speculative writers'. These people (who,

Mill implies, should know better), 'teach that things are right because they are right; because we feel them to be so'. They gull the public into believing that the things they *feel* to be right, provided that they are 'tolerably unanimous' in them, constitute an unquestionable standard to which everyone can be required to conform.

We know from an earlier essay of Mill's that one of these objectionable moralists was William Whewell (1794–1866), professor of moral philosophy at Cambridge from 1838 to 1855. Mill clashed at different times with Whewell on a variety of topics, from ethics to the philosophy of science (Bain describes him as having an 'antipathy' to the older writer).[6] In the essay 'Whewell on moral philosophy', published in 1852, he strongly criticized him for considering 'the moral feelings as their own justification'.[7] According to Whewell, if a moral feeling was shared by a large number of people, that was a good enough reason to presume its truth, and to disallow dissentient opinions. Mill thought that Jeremy Bentham had correctly rejected such a claim as one among 'many contrivances for avoiding the obligation of appealing to any external standard, and for prevailing upon the reader to accept of the author's sentiment or opinion as a reason for itself'.[8] Mill's own rebuttal of the idea is crisp and cogent:

> The appeal is always to something which is assumed to belong to all mankind. But it is not of much consequence whether the feeling which is set up as its own standard is the feeling of an individual human being, or of a multitude. A feeling is not proved to be right, and exempted from the need of justifying itself, because the writer or speaker is not only conscious of it in himself, but expects to find it in other people; because instead of saying 'I', he says 'you and I'.[9]

Mill's statement that when society interferes with personal conduct, it generally interferes 'wrongly, and in the wrong place' rests, then, on more than the empirical observation that individuals can be expected to know their own likes and dislikes better than other people. Mill is also making the deeper philosophical claim that the basis on which social intervention in individuals' lives is usually justified – namely, the presumption that what most members of society feel to be right must be right – is poorly founded. Even if every member of society, bar one, believed that a certain practice was morally wrong, that minority opinion might still be correct. Hence social interference in personal conduct is always wrong, because it rests upon an unsustainable assumption of moral infallibility. (Strictly speaking, a social intervention in individual conduct could theoretically be in the right place; but it would still be a wrong intervention, since the rightness of the place could not be known beyond all doubt).

Some readers at this point may think that Mill is taking moral scepticism too far. Where almost everyone feels that a particular kind of conduct is wrong, that might seem solid evidence that such conduct really is wrong. But Mill is not denying that our moral feelings provide some prima facie support for our moral opinions. If we feel that torturing children or stealing bread from the starving are wrong actions, then they probably are wrong. However, it is worth remembering some of the other moral feelings that people have also had in the past. Thus at various times people have felt that it was right to burn heretics and witches, to practise slavery, to expose unwanted children, and to punish severely wives who were disobedient to their husbands. Reflection on such cases supports Mill's contention that feeling is an unreliable guide to moral truth, and that it is dangerous to treat it as a final court of appeal. Following Bentham, Mill demands that our moral opinions should be answerable to some external standard – that is, that we should be able to articulate reasons for them that go beyond a statement of our gut feelings, attitudes or 'intuitions'. The provision of reasons for moral beliefs makes moral debate possible, from which truth and enlightenment can emerge. By contrast, dogmatically insisting that one already knows all the moral answers via one's feelings or intuitions forecloses the possibility of an escape from error should those feelings or intuitions be wrong. Mill's position is therefore better described as one of moral caution than of moral scepticism. His aim is not to persuade us that moral knowledge is unattainable, but to warn us against supposing that it can be securely attained by a purely subjective process unassisted by reason.

Before we leave this part of Mill's discussion, it is worth noting a further argument that he leaves undeveloped against the intervention by society in purely personal conduct. This fourth counter-argument cites the very strong reluctance that most adult people feel to being subjected to any form of control or compulsion in their own interests. No matter how well-intentioned such paternalism might be, it will normally be deeply disliked and resisted. John Gray remarks that 'weightier than any of his other interests, the individual has an interest in becoming or remaining an autonomous agent'.[10] This interest is incompatible with paternalistic interference with one's own choices. As John Skorupski explains, 'we vehemently resent being governed and directed for our own good' because 'we value the freedom to live our own lives, value it as a part of our good'.[11]

Mill would certainly have agreed. But he could usefully have made the argument more explicit (it is hinted at in some of the things he says about the pleasure we take in expressing our individuality). Himmelfarb suggests that Mill's doctrine of liberty could easily have taken a different tack from the point where he accepts the appropriateness of society's paternalistic management of children and young people. She thinks that Mill might have made the same concession in regard to those adults who, like children, are in danger of causing harm to themselves. This would have involved much less than 'the absolute denial of liberty and individuality', provided that it permitted only those controls 'whose legitimacy derived from long experience and an accepted body of "moral or prudential truth"'.[12] But Himmelfarb's idea that Mill may have teetered on the brink of allowing a much more widespread practice of paternalism is only credible if we assume, implausibly, that he failed to consider how strongly adult people resent being coerced. In view of that resentment, as Mill must have realized, it would be self-defeating as a device for increasing human happiness.

IV. 14–21: Examples of illegitimate control

One of the things that readers of *On Liberty* are apt to find frustrating up to this point is the paucity of examples provided by Mill in connection with his major claims. We have seen how the discussions of freedom of thought in chapter II and of individuality in chapter III proceed at a remarkably high level of abstraction. This feature of Mill's approach equally struck and frustrated his contemporaries, and it lies behind many of the perceptions expressed by his early reviewers of a lack of correspondence between Mill's large and sweeping claims of how things were and how they *really* were.

As if belatedly recognizing this weakness in his approach, Mill devotes the final pages of chapter IV and the whole of chapter V to a detailed study of the practical application of his doctrine of liberty in particular cases. We shall follow him in this study, and take the opportunity to reflect on the bearing of his ideas on some problems and contested issues of our own day.

But before we do that, it is worth pausing briefly to consider why the discussion of examples and specific instances is useful in works of moral or political theory (since *On Liberty* fits into both these categories, we can roll them together here). Two of the more obvious reasons for paying attention to them are the following:

(1) Examples help to clarify abstract or general claims. Sometimes it is hard to know what exactly is meant by a statement expressed in very general or abstract terms, and examples aid us in determining the speaker's or writer's intentions. Suppose that a person remarks to us that standards of social behaviour have deteriorated markedly over the last thirty years. In itself, this statement conveys merely a vague impression that the speaker is unhappy with some modern social trends. But we get a much clearer idea of what is meant if he explains that he is thinking of such changes as the decline in neighbourly relations between people living in the same locality; the fading of inhibitions against dropping litter, swearing in public or jumping queues; the privatizing of public spaces by the playing of excessively loud music or the insensitive use of mobile phones; the growth in the number of 'cheeky' youngsters; and the increase in discourteous driving on the roads. He may further illustrate these species of bad behaviour by adducing particular instances from his own experience. Supplying examples adds flesh to the bare bones of the original statement and reduces the possibility of mis-understanding. If we care to debate or dispute the speaker's generalization, we now know better what we are debating or disputing.

(2) Examples supply evidential support for generalizations. A second important function of examples is to provide evidence for our generalizations and theoretical statements. Imagine that we read in the newspaper that writers in a certain country who criticize the government are routinely persecuted by the police and secret service. In support of the claim, a long list of names is attached of individual writers who have been tortured or imprisoned. This makes the accusation more credible than if no names had been supplied, when we might have been inclined to suspect that the charge was a mischievous slander. (Even so, we may wish to check that the people on the list really have suffered persecution by the

government). If subsequently some other journalist provides examples of writers who have criticized the government and *not* suffered any penalties, then we may be brought to conclude that the original charge was false, or at least exaggerated.

Using examples for evidential purposes does, though, have a downside. Examples can be employed to mask the truth, as well as to reveal it. The careful selection of favourable and the omission of unfavourable examples is a common tactic of those who are keen to garner support for a controversial claim. It is also possible to skew the evidence by drawing on untypical, inaccurately described or poorly analysed instances. So the evidence offered by examples, like any other kind of evidence, needs to be treated with caution. When examples are cited for or against a thesis we should always ask whether there are others which point in a different direction. Otherwise we risk believing the thesis, as Mill expressed it, 'in the manner of a prejudice' (II. 43).

Besides (1) and (2), there is a further very important reason why moral and political philosophy should be concerned with the particular and specific. Citing examples to clarify a thesis, or to provide it with evidential support, treats those individual cases, so to speak, as means to an end – that of furthering our general or theoretical knowledge. But that is not the only kind of knowledge we are interested in having. We live in a world of particulars – particular people, events, processes, situations, relationships, experiences, emotions – which we need to sort and classify, compare and differentiate, assess and evaluate. Knowledge of the particular is thus not only a means to knowledge of the general; it is also an end in itself. One of the reasons why knowledge of general principles is important is precisely that we can apply it to make predictions about and provide explanations of particular instances. We descend from the general to the particular because we do not spend our lives among abstractions; we want to know how to act in *this* situation, or what judgement to make about *that*. Mankind cannot live by pure knowledge alone: applied knowledge is needed too.

We can now turn to Mill's own discussion of examples in the final paragraphs of chapter IV. They are intended to illustrate and support the important psychological thesis that 'to extend the bounds of what may be called moral police, until it encroaches on the most unquestionably legitimate liberty of the individual, is one of the most universal of all human propensities' (IV. 13). On Mill's theory of human nature, we find it immensely hard to keep our noses out of other people's business when we feel that their conduct offends against our own moral or religious values. Of this regrettable trait 'abundant instances' may be offered, of which Mill selects seven:

(i) Muslims (Mill calls them 'Mahomedans' or 'Mussulmans') greatly dislike the idea of eating pork, which they regard as the flesh of an unclean animal, and ban its consumption in their own countries (IV. 14);

(ii) Spaniards 'consider it a gross impiety, offensive in the highest degree to the Supreme Being, to worship him in any other manner than the Roman Catholic'; they consequently forbid all other kinds of worship in their country (IV. 15);

(iii) at various times in Britain and New England, people of a puritan persuasion 'have endeavoured, with considerable success, to put down all public, and nearly all private, amusements: especially music, dancing, public games, or other assemblages for purposes of diversion, or the theatre' (IV. 16);

(iv) a majority of people in the United States disapprove of a showy or costly style of living, as a result of which 'in many parts of the Union it is really difficult for a person possessing a very large income to find any mode of spending it which will not incur popular disapprobation' (IV. 17);

(v) in both Britain and America, an energetic temperance movement has sought to ban the production, sale and consumption of alcohol, and in nearly half of the United States people are forbidden by law from making any but medicinal uses of fermented beverages (Mill's reference here is to the so-called Maine laws, named for the state which first introduced prohibition in 1851) (IV. 19);

(vi) Sabbatarian legislation already enforces the suspension of industry on one day in the week, and those who believe that the Sabbath should be kept holy continue to call for further restrictions on Sunday amusements (including the visiting of museums) and travel (IV. 20);

(vii) the 'remarkable phenomenon of Mormonism' has attracted fierce denunciation and active persecution, and many of the early adherents of the new religion have been murdered or forced into exile. The chief ground of objection is the Mormon habit of polygamous marriage, which 'seems to excite unquenchable animosity when practised by persons who speak English and profess to be a kind of Christians' (IV. 21).

These diverse examples all represent the characteristic unwillingness of human beings to live and let live. Each of them involves what Mill describes as the unwarranted interference with 'the personal tastes and self-regarding concerns of individuals' (IV. 14). What one chooses to eat and drink, how one worships one's God or spends one's money, the pastimes one indulges in (and when), the form of marriage one contracts with a willing partner or partners, are all matters, Mill thinks, that fall within the self-regarding area. They are therefore off-limits to the public, and individuals are entitled to resist the efforts of officious souls who try to make them conform to what *they* consider the appropriate norms. Mill allows that those who seek to make others do what they think they should are motivated by sincere feelings, and that they may be deeply pained by witnessing, or even thinking about, the conduct they deplore. But he denies that these are reasons for letting them have their way. For once it is granted that 'all mankind have a vested interest in each other's moral, intellectual, and even physical perfection, to be defined by each claimant according to his own standard', then individual liberty is doomed (IV.19).

Mill's outright rejection of all forms of social interference in individuals' self-regarding concerns once again presupposes that a clear line can be drawn between self- and other-regarding conduct. That there is *not* always a sharp line of demarcation is apparent from the discussion in paragraph 19 of the arguments offered by the United Kingdom Alliance for the total legal prohibition of the consumption of alcohol. Mill quotes from a correspondence in *The Times* newspaper in October 1856 between the Alliance's secretary, William Pope, and Lord E.H. Stanley, MP. (Mill's presentation may give the misleading impression that he is criticizing Stanley, but it is actually the arguments of the unnamed Pope that are the focus of attack). Pope claims that a number of his 'social rights' are threatened by others' consumption of strong drink, e.g. his right of security (since the use of alcohol generates public disorder) and his 'right to free moral and intellectual development' by its 'weakening and demoralising society', from which he has 'a right to claim mutual aid and intercourse'. Mill will have none of this; to concede to the Alliance that anyone has such rights, he argues, would be tantamount to allowing 'that it is the absolute social right of every individual, that every other individual shall act in every respect exactly as he ought; that whosoever fails thereof in the smallest particular violates my social right, and entitles me to demand from the legislature the removal of the grievance'. But this is an unlikely and overblown construal of Pope's position, possibly motivated by Mill's uncomfortable awareness that the Alliance is right to say that the drinker's (or rather, the drunkard's) behaviour has potentially bad consequences for others besides himself. Rather than make the implausible claim that the Alliance is asserting a right that everyone else should act 'exactly as he ought', Mill would do better to resort, as he has done on other occasions, to a more utilitarian style of argument, according to which the social and individual benefits of allowing everyone the liberty to indulge their desire for alcoholic beverages outweigh the attendant disbenefits.

The issue dividing Mill and the UKA pinpoints the more general problem facing Mill that much of the behaviour that he refers to as 'self-regarding' is far from being purely so. It would be hard to argue that John's taking a railway journey on a Sunday or Mary's visiting the theatre during Lent have any potential negative impact on anyone else. But even these are not entirely self-regarding acts, since both involve interactions with other people (e.g. train-drivers, actors, ticket-sellers). Instead of claiming that we should be at liberty to do whatever we want in purely self-regarding areas, which are likely to be very few, Mill might more wisely have placed *all* the weight on the harm principle, and held that we should be free to please ourselves so long as we cause no harmful consequences to others. So while Mary's visiting the theatre may not be a wholly self-regarding act, its legitimacy is assured by its harmlessness.

But, unfortunately, there is a further source of difficulty, and one that we have already touched on in Part III, chapter II. As C.L. Ten remarks, Mill was ultra-sensitive to the harm caused to an individual by other individuals or society, but inclined to ignore 'the cohesive effects of having shared values and institutions' and consequently 'the harm to society caused by the undermining of these institutions and the violation of the shared values'.[13] This combination of sensitivity and insensitivity might be suspected to underlie Mill's first example of intolerance, that of the prohibition in Islamic countries of the eating of pork. On Mill's thinking, if a Christian visitor to a Muslim land were prevented from consuming pork, this would be an illegitimate infringement of his liberty, since his eating habits are a self-regarding concern and entirely harmless to other people. While it might be polite for the visitor to desist from doing something that his hosts find offensive (there are, after all, plenty of other things he could eat instead), it would be social tyranny for them to insist that he avoids pig's flesh. Against this it can be argued that a society has a right to enforce those values and practices which it considers fundamental to its self-image and idea of the good; also that it is not *obviously* true that an individual's right to do what she wants will always outweigh the public's right to prohibit behaviour which runs contrary to its basic principles. For whatever offends against these may be held to chip away at the cement which binds society together, and that is plainly a very considerable harm.

Intriguingly, this is a position which Mill himself had once explicitly maintained. In his 1840 essay on Coleridge he had argued that social cohesiveness could not exist without 'the feeling of allegiance, or loyalty', and that this depended on there being *'something* which is settled, something permanent, and not to be called into question'; in all stable political societies there had to be 'something which men agreed in holding sacred'. This something might be a God or gods, a particular person (such as a monarch), or a system of laws, liberties, practices or institutions.[14] It is probable that the Mill of *On Liberty* still believed that a measure of agreement in values and practices was needed for social cohesion, though he had reduced his estimate of the amount of this required. If Mill in 1840 sounds in some sympathy with Devlin's view that social well-being requires the enforcement of a common moral code, Mill in 1859 assuredly does not. Ten makes the persuasive suggestion that Mill was now prepared to countenance a limited degree of instability in social life as the price of allowing a more substantial individual liberty.[15] Even in the earlier essay Mill had voiced the hope that future states of society would be bound together by a feeling of allegiance to 'the principles of individual freedom and political and social equality'.[16] From Mill's point of view, this would evidently be an ideal solution to the problem of reconciling social stability and individual liberty.

Jonathan Riley, defending Mill, points out that it is possible for an individual *both* to absorb many 'popular norms and beliefs' *and* still '[be] capable of deciding to choose differently than the majority of his fellows'.[17] A person can be at once socially situated and independently-minded. Mill recognized this possibility, thereby avoiding the absurdity of imagining that an individual, in pursuing self-development, can 'transcend altogether the social context in which he finds himself'.[18] But while Riley's construal of Mill's position is convincing, it serves, too, to indicate where the problems are likely to arise. Since individuals are never 'radically unsituated' but live as members of society, their own well-being is bound up in that of the wider community. It is therefore in their interests to cooperate in the enterprise of preserving that community in a flourishing condition. But this may require them to make compromises between their individual aspirations and projects and those of society. A person may love the taste of pork yet reasonably be expected to forego it when it is believed to offend the community's patron deity. In treating the issue as if it concerned merely an individual's culinary preferences, Mill forgets that one man's meat is another man's sacrilege. (Just how seriously Muslims took the ban on pork was made violently apparent by the events in India in 1857–9, when the refusal of the Muslim soldiers of the East India Company to use rifle cartridges they believed to be greased with pork fat gave rise to what became known in Britain as the 'Indian Mutiny').

Several of Mill's examples testify to his strongly-held conviction that religion was a strictly private matter and that people should not try to impose their own religious practices, abstentions or ethical code on anyone else. He deplored the 'determination not to tolerate others doing what is permitted by their religion, because it is not permitted by the persecutor's religion'. Yet he candidly acknowledged that such behaviour was often driven by 'a belief that God not only abominates the act of the misbeliever, but will not hold us guiltless if we leave him unmolested' (IV. 20). For those who hold this belief, upholding God's law is a moral duty which must trump any other putative duties to leave individuals free to please themselves. Mill took the line that God or the gods could look after themselves ('*Deorum injuriae Diis curae*' – 'Injuries to the gods are the gods' own concern') (IV. 20). But not everyone shared that view, or shares it today. Ever since biblical times many people have believed that neglecting to enforce God's commands risks alienating the divine favour, and that religion therefore cannot be treated as a purely private affair. Raymond Geuss observes that where we draw the division between public and private spheres turns crucially on 'what sorts of things we think need regulating or caring for'; and orthodox Muslims would draw that line in a quite different place to Mill.[19] For the latter, religion is a wholly private matter; for the former, an individual's religious practices, or lack of them, are an issue of intense common concern and so fall within the sphere of public regulation.

Before we move on to Mill's final chapter, it is worth noting a seeming inconsistency between a view expressed at the end of chapter IV and a position taken earlier in the book. Mill remarks in regard to his final example of intolerance, the vicious persecution of members of the Mormon church, that while it would be perfectly acceptable to send missionaries to persuade people to give up this 'alleged new revelation', 'the product of palpable imposture', it would be wrong to mount, as some have recommended, a '*civili-zade*' against them. Although Mill considers that Mormonism, with its practice of polygamous marriage, represents 'a retrograde step in civilisation', he is 'not aware that any community has a right to force another to be civilised' (IV. 21). Things might be different if Mormonism posed a threat to civilization – though even that might not be an adequate reason for *forcibly* suppressing it, since any civilization liable to crumble when confronted by barbarism must be so degenerate as scarcely to be worth saving. But Mill's rejection of a 'civilizade' against the Mormons may seem in conflict with the claim made in chapter I that '[d]espotism is a legitimate mode of dealing with barbarians, provided the end be their improvement, and the means justified by actually effecting that end' (I. 10).

But perhaps these passages can be reconciled. Mill proposes, in chapter I, that the principle of liberty has 'no application to any state of things *anterior to the time when mankind have become capable of being improved by free and equal discussion*' (I. 10; emphasis added). Despite Mill's implied classification of Mormonism, at IV. 21, as a species of barbarism, he may have thought (as his reference to the sending of missionaries suggests) that the Mormons were still sufficiently within the pale of civilization to be able to be 'improved by free and equal discussion'. Having made the grade, they were entitled to be subjected to persuasion rather than coercion. But Mill's closing remarks in chapter IV are interesting too for showing clearly his belief that civilizations are not intrinsically stable structures and are capable of retrogression. (If things get sufficiently bad, he suggests, it may be best for a civilization to be 'destroyed and regenerated ... by energetic barbarians' [IV. 21].) These observations on the fragility of civilization reinforce the moral drawn by Mill more explicitly in 'Coleridge' than in *On Liberty*, that stable societies require something settled and permanent to focus the loyalty of their members – something which people agree to hold sacred and which is 'in the common estimation placed beyond discussion'.[20] This 'something' might, in principle, be a respect for the value of individuality. But more often it is not, and where it is not, the question arises of how much individual liberty Mill would be prepared to see traded away as the price of maintaining social stability.

Study Questions

1. What duties, if any, does society have a right to exact from its members?
2. How cogent is Mill's distinction of self- and other-regarding spheres?
3. Is it ever permissible to force someone to listen to good advice?
4. Is Mill right to claim that we have a natural desire to control others? Discuss with illustrations.
5. Does the legal prohibition of the use of hard drugs for recreational purposes constitute an illegitimate infringement of individual liberty?
6. How important to social well-being is the existence of common moral values, and does society have a right to enforce these?

CHAPTER V: APPLICATIONS

V. 1–6: Illustrations of the doctrine of liberty

Chapter V is the second-longest of *On Liberty* and is intended, as Mill explains in its first paragraph, to provide 'specimens of illustration' of the major principles defended in the book. These will serve to 'bring into greater clearness the meaning and limits of the two maxims' which form the 'entire doctrine' of the work, and 'assist the judgement in holding the balance between them, in the cases where it appears doubtful which of them is applicable to the case' (V. 1). Several of the themes and arguments of the chapter had appeared earlier in Book V, chapter 11 of *The Principles of Political Economy* (first edition 1848), which paves the way for *On Liberty* in its uncompromising claim that 'there is a circle around every human being which no government, be it that of one, of a few, or of the many, ought to be permitted to overstep'.[1]

It may surprise the reader that the 'one very simple principle' of chapter I has now become two maxims, but the change is presentational rather than substantial:

> The maxims are, first, that the individual is not accountable to society for his actions, in so far as these concern the interests of no person but himself. ... Secondly, that for such actions as are prejudicial to the interests of others, the individual is accountable, and may be subjected either to social or to legal punishment, if society is of opinion that the one or the other is requisite for its protection (V. 2).

These maxims spell out the dual practical import of the 'one very simple principle': we may only interfere with the conduct of an individual when it harms, or threatens to harm, the interests of other people, and *not* when the agent's own interests alone are at stake.

Society may not interfere with an individual's conduct unless it damages, or threatens to damage, the interests of others. But it may sometimes not intervene even then. As we have already seen, Mill regards the prospect of a person's conduct harming others as a necessary rather than a sufficient condition for the permissibility of external interference. Mill now points out that many aspects of social life are competitive, and that in pursuing their own legitimate ends people will often inevitably cause pain or loss to others:

> Whoever succeeds in an overcrowded profession, or in a competitive examination; whoever is preferred to another in any contest for an object which both desire, reaps benefit from the loss of others, from their wasted effort and their disappointment. But it is, by common admission, better for the general interest of mankind, that persons should pursue their objects undeterred by this sort of consequences (V. 3).

If Smith and Jones compete for a job and Smith is appointed, then Smith's success harms Jones's interests (assuming that nothing else would have prevented the latter's getting the job). Mill, in a frankly utilitarian argument, contends that the good of society requires that such forms of harm be tolerated. There is no better way of organizing many social institutions, and it is also more respectful of individuals' freedom to allow them to compete for many contested goods than to have those goods allocated by some central authority. Society should merely adjudicate the fairness of such competitions. It should admit 'no right, either legal or moral, in the disappointed competitors to immunity from this kind of suffering'; but it has the duty to ensure that no fraud, treachery or force are employed to skew the outcomes (V. 3).

One question that Mill does not address in *On Liberty* is whether society might reasonably go further than this and seek to ensure that candidates for desirable jobs, offices and privileges compete on a completely level playing-field. How pro-active should a government and its agencies be in tackling disadvantage and promoting social equality, so that anyone who wishes to may take part in such competitions with a reasonable chance of winning? When Smith is offered the job, his victory over Brown may have been fairly won but there may be other people who would also have applied for it had they not felt excluded by their 'wrong' gender, social class or ethnic group. In a just society, competitions have not only to be fairly conducted but be open to all who have the ability to compete so long as their entry is not impeded by artificial barriers.

US President Lyndon B. Johnson observed in a famous speech to black graduates at Howard University in 1965 that 'You do not take a man who, for years, has been hobbled by chains, bring him to the starting line of a race, saying "You are free to compete with all the others", and still justly believe you have been completely fair'. Affirmative action was needed in support of groups who had historically been disadvantaged by poverty, lack of civil rights and mediocre educational provision. It was not enough to throw open the gates of opportunity but 'all our citizens must have the ability to walk through those gates'.[2] Mill would undoubtedly have been sympathetic to Johnson's objectives but it is less clear that he would have wanted the state to play the major role in righting such historic wrongs as those of the black population of the American deep south. Mill did not believe that governments were the most efficient or appropriate providers of social benefits. Their function, rather, was to promote fair competition by removing any non-natural obstacles in the path of individuals. However, sometimes the best, or even the only, way, to remove such obstacles is by providing new goods and services, e.g. building better schools for the educationally deprived. Whilst Mill would probably have accepted the need in some cases for this kind of 'affirmative action', his reluctance to put excessive power in the hands of the central authority would have made him uneasy with the idea of the state or its agencies supplying the benefits. With Mill it amounted almost to an article of faith that state intervention increased the risk of state domination. (We shall discuss later in this chapter some more of the reasons that underlay this belief).

Mill's rooted dislike of artificial impediments to individuals' advancement also makes it unlikely that he would have endorsed any practices of positive discrimination in favour of people who had previously been disadvantaged. The problem with positively discriminating in the interests of some is that it necessarily involves negatively discriminating against others who are denied the same head-start. It is typical of Mill that when, in *The Subjection of Women* (1869) he strongly condemned the legal and conventional hindrances that still lay in the path of women's self- and social development, he stopped short of calling for women to be given any kind of compensatory advantages that were not enjoyed by men.

Mill's belief in the value of fair competition is further exhibited in his espousal of 'the so-called doctrine of Free Trade' (V. 4). In *On Liberty* Mill says little about economic affairs, since he had already published a massive two-volume work on the subject, the *Principles of Political Economy*, in 1848; his remarks on strictly economic issues in the later work are contained within a page or so. Mill describes trade as being 'free' when governments refrain from fixing prices or regulating the process of manufacture. But Mill's concept of free trade is less radical than that of some of his contemporaries. Recognizing the social dangers attendant on *laissez-faire* capitalism, he sees an important role for government in controlling 'sanitary precautions, or arrangements to protect workpeople employed in dangerous occupations'. Interventions by the state to protect those who would be vulnerable to exploitation under a wholly unregulated form of free trade are justified under the harm principle. The argument in favour of leaving trade as free as is compatible with the provision of some minimal safety-nets is again essentially a utilitarian one, focused on the public good:

[I]t is now recognised, though not till after a long struggle, that both the cheapness and the good quality of commodities are most effectually provided for by leaving the producers and sellers perfectly free, under the sole check of equal freedom to the buyers for supplying themselves elsewhere. (V. 4)

Provided that monopolies are avoided in manufacture or supply, Mill believes that everyone will benefit from the existence of a capitalist free market, which can be expected to produce cheaper, better and more plentiful goods than the alternatives.

Mill offers the further argument for free trade that people have a right to buy and consume what they wish, on the usual proviso that they cause no harm to others. So the Maine Laws should be repealed so that Americans can buy alcohol, and the prohibition lifted on the importation of opium to China (a trade which had formerly been largely in the hands of Mill's erstwhile employer, the British East India Company). While the controversial issue of the Chinese opium trade receives only passing mention, Mill spends longer on the question of whether the police or other authorities should have the right to prevent the sale of poisons. This, he thinks, is worth discussion because it raises a new question of 'how far liberty may legitimately be invaded for the prevention of crime, or of accident'. If poisons were never bought for any purpose except the commission of murder, it would be undeniably reasonable to forbid their manufacture and sale. But the problem is that they may be 'wanted not only for innocent but for useful purposes, and restrictions cannot be imposed in the one case without operating in the other' (V. 5).

Although Mill is not very explicit about the kinds of poisons he means, he appears chiefly to be thinking of medicinal drugs, such as laudanum (an alcoholic tincture of opium), which are dangerous if taken in large quantities. (He may have in mind too the use of poisons for exterminating rats and other vermin, which abounded in the more squalid parts of nineteenth-century towns and cities). Since he objects that requiring that poisons should only be sold under the certificate of a medical practitioner 'would make it sometimes impossible, always expensive, to obtain the article for legitimate uses', it is possible he is glancing obliquely at recreational drug-use – though even an apostle of liberty such as Mill would be unlikely to think this one of the 'useful purposes' of poison. The solution he finally recommends is a compromise: the over-the-counter sale of poisonous substances should be permitted under the two conditions that they are clearly labelled as dangerous (since 'the buyer cannot wish not to know that the thing he possesses has poisonous qualities'), and that all sales are recorded by the seller in a register (V. 5).

Because society has a right 'to ward off crimes against itself by antecedent precautions', Mill proposes that people who have shown themselves liable to commit offences when in certain self-induced conditions such as drunkenness, or to shirk their legal duties to others (as an idle man might neglect to support his children), may properly be subjected to special sanctions or pressure that are not attached to their conditions (drunkenness, idleness) as a matter of course (V. 6). A good modern example of the kind of preventive restrictions on liberty which Mill is defending is the issuing in the UK of Anti-Social Behaviour Orders, or ASBOs, which seek to control known troublemakers by imposing curfews on them or limiting their access to public places. Although the use of ASBOs is occasionally criticized for unfairly punishing people for their prospective rather than their actual offences, Mill would undoubtedly respond that since the public has a right to protect itself, individuals who have shown themselves liable to cause harm to others cannot justly protest when their liberty to do so is curtailed.

This is an appropriate place to pause to say a little more about Mill's concept of liberty, and to consider certain problems which it faces. In paragraph 6, Mill writes that 'liberty consists in doing what one desires'. As Bernard Williams has remarked, this cannot be quite what Mill means, since, taken literally, it implies that one is unfree whenever one simply chooses not to do what one desires. What Mill evidently means is that one is free when one has the capacity to do what one desires (a doctrine identical, Williams notes, to Locke's that 'Liberty, 'tis plain, consists in a power to do or not to do; to do or forbear doing as we will').[3] Williams labels the condition of being unobstructed by other human beings from doing what one wants 'primitive freedom'.[4] Freedom of this primitive kind, though, is not very attractive as a political value. One reason for that has already been identified by Mill himself: social life involves unavoidable and legitimate competition between individuals who can only satisfy their own wants at the expense of others. When Smith gets the job that Jones would have liked, Jones cannot complain that Smith has treated him unjustly by preventing him from obtaining what he wants. Whilst Jones's primitive freedom has been restricted by Smith, his rightful liberty has not. It would be absurd for the state to step in and punish Smith for flouting Jones's desire. So the kind of individual liberty that will be protected in a just society cannot be primitive freedom. But in that case, Mill needs to tell us more clearly what it is.

Mill's casual definition of liberty in terms of the capacity to do what one wants is unsatisfactory too for another reason. To say that people should be allowed to do whatever they want is to skate over the fact that people's capacity for autonomous choice can be impeded by internal as well as external obstacles. For instance, someone addicted to a drug may feel unable to give it up even though no one else is forcing him to keep on taking it. It is quite possible to want alcohol or opium or heroin, and yet want *not* to want it. But the possibility of a divergence between our first- and our second-order desires (i.e. desires which have other desires as their objects) is overlooked by Mill. He does not see that 'getting what we want' is sometimes bad for us, or that primitive freedom, in the sense of the capacity to satisfy our first-order wants, is actually a form of unfreedom when our second-order desires not to be governed by those first-order desires (e.g. to have another drink or another shot of heroin) are powerless to overcome them. Writing about the conditions for autonomous choice, Charles Taylor fills in some of the gaps that Mill leaves:

> the capacities relevant to freedom must involve some self-awareness, self-understanding, moral discrimination, and self-control, otherwise their exercise couldn't amount to freedom in the sense of self-direction, and this being so, we can fail to be free because these internal conditions are not realized. But where this happens, where, for instance, we are quite self-deceived, or utterly fail to discriminate properly the ends we seek, or have lost self-control, we can quite easily be doing what we want in the sense of what we can identify as our wants, without being free; indeed, we can be further entrenching our unfreedom.[5]

It is intriguing in this context that Mill condemns the British government's prohibition of the trade in opium to China as an unwarrantable interference with the liberty of individuals to decide for themselves whether to purchase a recreational drug for their personal use. Opium-eating, like drinking alcohol, is for Mill an activity situated firmly within the self-regarding area. It should therefore become subject to external restraint or control only where it has harmful consequences for other people (avid opium eaters, like hopeless drunkards, may culpably fail to discharge duties they owe to other people). Mill probably underestimated the depth of the social crisis into which the widespread use of opium had plunged parts of China, and which had led to the Chinese autho-rities' protest against the trade. (It was, incidentally, the British government's initial refusal to stop the opium traffic that resulted in the fighting of the 'Opium Wars', one of the least honourable chapters in the history of British imperialism, though one that Mill seems to have found surprisingly untroubling.[6]) But he seems also to have had an imperfect understanding of the nature of drug addiction, and of the damage that addiction can do to personal autonomy. People addicted to opium, like those addicted to heroin or crack cocaine today, were often incapable of kicking a habit which they knew was doing them immense personal harm. Later in chapter V, Mill argues that it would be perfectly proper to stop someone's selling himself into slavery because 'by selling himself for a slave, he abdicates his liberty; he foregoes any future use of it by that single act'. 'The principle of freedom', he explains, 'cannot require that he should be free not to be free. It is not freedom to be allowed to alienate his freedom' (V. 11). But he fails to consider that analogous reasoning would justify the prohibition of the sale to individuals of addictive drugs which, once they become enslaved to them, seriously curtail their capacity for further autonomous choice.

V. 7: Violations of good manners

We come next to one of the most problematic paragraphs in *On Liberty*. There are many acts, Mill writes,

> which, being directly injurious only to the agents themselves, ought not to be legally interdicted [i.e. forbidden], but which, if done publicly, are a violation of good manners, and coming thus within the category of offences against others, may rightly be prohibited. Of this kind are offences against decency, on which it is unnecessary to dwell, the rather as they are only connected

indirectly with our subject, the objection to publicity being equally strong in the case of many actions not in themselves condemnable, nor supposed to be so. (V. 7)

This passage raises several puzzles. A minor one is that it is not clear why Mill thinks that 'offences against decency' should be injurious to those who are behaving indecently. It is also unobvious why such offences are 'only connected indirectly with our subject' if they constitute genuine offences against others. Most perplexingly, the notion that violations of good manners may reasonably be prohibited seems hard to align with Mill's earlier insistence that we cannot expect to be protected against things which offend us but do us no actual harm. If I find your religious beliefs or mode of worship objectionable, or dislike the music you play, the clothes you wear or your habit of dropping your aitches, the problem is with me and not you; I have no right to insist that you change your ways and make them conform with my ideas of what is right and proper. Or so Mill has been telling us so far.

The legal philosopher Ronald Dworkin has distinguished between the preferences that people have in regard to the allocation of goods or opportunities to themselves, and those which they have about the allocation of goods or opportunities to others. Legislators, he argues, who have the task of allocating the available goods and opportunities, must take note only of the former, 'personal', preferences, and ignore the latter 'external' ones.[7] This distinction can be extended to encompass preferences regarding one's own and other people's behaviour. On this basis, the fact that a majority of people believe that others' practising pre-marital sex, or bowing the head at the name of Jesus, or wearing red tee-shirts, is wrong is no reason to forbid any of these practices, since the preferences concerned are of the external kind. Of course, where people are pained at the thought that others are doing the things they disapprove of or dislike, they will have a personal preference not to be subjected to that discomfort. Yet this is one personal preference that legislators should ignore, since it is grounded solely in an irrelevant external preference. Dworkin's view seems very close to the view we might have ascribed to Mill – until we come to paragraph V. 7.

Mill gives no examples of the 'violations of good manners' which he considers may be forbidden and – presumably – punished if they are persisted in. But he is probably thinking of activities of a kind likely to cause embarrassment, such as going nude in public, and of what Joel Feinberg has termed 'harmless immoralities', e.g. performing an overt sexual act in the market-place. Some writers have sought to defend Mill's position by drawing attention to the fact that sensitive souls may be caused great pain by being exposed to such activities. On their view, something that Feinberg might describe as a *harmless* immorality may not really be so harmless after all, if people who witness it find it very upsetting. But this defence has the snag that, while the beholders' pain may be genuine and acute, it only arises because they hold a particular external preference. So banning the activity in question on the ground that it causes them pain is open to the objection that they only feel the pain because they are not prepared to mind their own business.

Feinberg and Ten, however, believe that this objection can be turned if we apply what Feinberg calls 'the standard of reasonable avoidability'.[8] Ten points out that there is a big difference between performing an overt sexual act in a crowded market-place and on a secluded beach; while both are public places, the latter, unlike the former, can easily be avoided by people who do not want to witness such acts. If a couple who wish to perform a sexual act under the blue sky insist on doing so in the market-place instead of on the lonely beach (either because they desire to give offence or because they are indifferent to other people's feelings), their behaviour can then be described as an 'offensive nuisance'. According to Ten, '[i]f such acts may be prohibited, it is not simply because they are offensive, but because they are offensive nuisances'.[9] Feinberg writes in similar vein that:

> No one has a right to protection from the state against offensive experiences if he can easily and effectively avoid those experiences with no unreasonable effort or inconvenience. If [however] a nude person enters a public bus and takes a seat near the front, there may be no effective way whatever for the other patrons to avoid intensely shameful embarrassment (or other insupportable feelings) short of leaving the bus themselves, which would be an unreasonable inconvenience. Similarly, obscene remarks over a loudspeaker, homosexual bill boards in Times Square, pornographic handbills thrust into the hands of passing pedestrians all fail to be reasonably avoidable.[10]

(Feinberg adds that the 'offense principle' as set out above gives no warrant to the suppression of obscene books, which no one need look at unless they wish to).

Although it may be reading too much into Mill's use of the phrase 'violation of good manners' to suppose that he anticipates Feinberg and Ten's position precisely, it is noteworthy that Ten's 'offensive nuisances' can be said to offend against good manners in a way that acts which meet the avoidability standard, such as making love out of the public eye on a secluded beach, cannot. Mill, as a utilitarian, must regard all unnecessary causation of pain as a bad thing. So while his desire for a wide sphere of individual liberty prompts him to resist the imposition of restrictions and controls based upon the external preferences that people, even where they are in a majority, may happen to have, his brief remarks at V. 7 are suggestive of a compromise position whereby restraints may be placed on those who cause needless and avoidable pain by their disregard of good manners. Jonathan Wolff reminds us that Mill has no belief in 'the idea of abstract right, as a thing independent of utility' (I. 11).[11] On a theory of rights founded on the notion of utility, it is implausible to suppose that people could have a right to cause others unnecessary pain. Therefore, thinks Wolff, Mill can consistently argue that a public display of indecency (one which fails to meet Feinberg's 'unavoidability standard') may be banned; '[t]o use a phrase common in the condemnation of indecent or other ill-mannered behaviour: it is "so unnecessary" '.[12]

But is there not a danger that if we allow censorious people's external preferences to count to the extent of prohibiting 'violations of good manners', it will be hard to hold the line against allowing them to dictate also what may be permissibly done away from the public gaze? As Wolff remarks, 'the sight of something is not necessarily a worse harm than the bare knowledge that it is taking place'; for some people, the very thought that a couple may be having sex on a secluded beach, or watching obscene videos in the privacy of their own home, may be a source of great pain.[13] It may seem arbitrary to propose that people's displeasure at witnessing indecent acts is a relevant factor in determining whether those acts may legitimately be banned, but not their displeasure at the thought of the indecent acts which they do not see.

Yet there are utilitarian arguments for the view that a dividing line drawn where Feinberg, Ten, Wolff and (apparently) Mill wish to draw it is in roughly the right place. Informing people that they may not perform certain kinds of act in a frequented place is far less of a curtailment of their liberty and threat to their happiness than telling them that they may not perform those acts at all. Before homosexual relations between consenting males was legalized in Britain in 1967, it would have been hard to argue that the pain, frustration and affront caused to gay men by the existence and implementation of the legal ban were outweighed by the pleasure felt by those who were glad that the law was taking a tough stand against 'immorality'. Moreover, a resolute attempt to 'enforce morals' would require a degree of intrusion into private life by the police or similar agencies that even the prudish or morally conservative could scarcely find tolerable (imagine a CCTV camera being installed in every bedroom). Whether any system of surveillance, even one aided by the latest technological gadgetry, would be very successful at detecting forbidden behaviour is in any case moot in view of human ingenuity at 'beating the system'. What is not moot is that such a regimen would be very unpleasant to live under, for saints and sinners alike.

V. 8–10: Limits of paternal government

In the following three paragraphs Mill raises two further questions concerning the proper role of government and society in regard to the protection of individual interests. Although no new issues of principle are introduced, this part of the discussion articulates some further practical implications of Mill's understanding of liberty.

The first question is whether individuals should be free to instigate other individuals to behave in ways which are either morally or physically harmful to the self (interestingly, Mill's discussion barely distinguishes between these two forms of harm). 'The case of a person who solicits another to do an act', Mill points out, 'is not strictly a case of self-regarding conduct. To give advice or inducements to any one is a social act, and may, therefore, like actions in general which affect others, be supposed amenable to social control' (V. 8). Yet if people are free to make their own decisions in matters that concern themselves, it seems to follow that they must be free to go to others for advice or assistance. However, Mill is disturbed by the fact that most of the people who supply services of the kinds in question do so not out of charity but for wholly self-interested reasons. 'Fornication, for example, must be tolerated, and so must gambling; but should a person be free to be a pimp, or to keep a gambling-house?' (V. 8). The issue is whether it is right to allow some persons to make a living by providing the opportunities for others to behave badly.

Mill allows that there are arguments on both sides. There *is* a case, he believes, for banning such disreputable establishments as brothels or gambling-houses, which exploit human weakness and encourage immoral behaviour for purely commercial motives. Nonetheless, there would be a 'moral anomaly' in 'punishing the accessary [*sic*], when the principal is (and must be) allowed to go free; of fining or imprisoning the procurer, but not the fornicator – the gambling-house keeper, but not the gambler'. Mill's recommendation is a compromise (or more unkindly, a fudge): governments should exert a measure of control of pimps, gambling-house proprietors and 'dealers in strong drinks', but allow them to pursue their trades so long as they 'conduct their operations with a certain degree of secrecy and mystery' and take care to keep the peace (V.8).

The second question is 'whether the State, while it permits, should nevertheless indirectly discourage conduct which it deems contrary to the best interests of the agent' – for instance, seek to reduce the amount of drunkenness by placing heavy taxes on alcohol and limiting the number of outlets at which it can be bought. Mill objects that taxing stimulants in order to discourage their use 'is a measure differing only in degree from their entire prohibition; and would be justifiable only if that were justifiable' – which it is not (V. 9). Yet there is a practical consideration which can take up some of the slack in the argument. Since any government needs to raise money through taxation if it is to continue functioning, it is better for it to tax 'the commodities the consumers can best spare' rather than essentials. Taxing alcohol is therefore preferable to taxing bread or clothing. So though the state should not tax alcohol with the specific aim of discouraging drinking, it is justified in raising tax revenue from sales of an item which is not a necessity (V. 9).

Mill adds that it is sensible to confine the power of selling alcohol 'to persons of known or vouched-for respectability of conduct' who are able and willing to keep good order in the premises they manage. Where 'breaches of the peace repeatedly take place through the connivance or incapacity of the keeper of the house', the licence to sell alcohol may be withdrawn (V. 10). But it is wrong to attempt to create a more temperate society by restricting the number of beer and spirit houses or making them more difficult of access. Such measures would unfairly penalise people who drank responsibly and moderately and it is objectionable paternalism to treat people as if they were 'children or savages'. 'This is not', Mill declares, 'the principle on which the labouring classes are professedly governed in any free country.' There must be no 'system of despotic, or what is called paternal, government' which seeks to interfere with individuals' self-regarding conduct (V. 10).

V. 11: The scope of voluntary engagements

To its early readership, paragraph V. 11 must have appeared one of the more politically and morally radical passages in *On Liberty*. Mill starts by reminding us that 'the liberty of the individual, in things wherein the individual is alone concerned, implies a corresponding liberty in any number of individuals to regulate by mutual agreement such things as regard them jointly'. What, though, should happen if one of the parties to an agreement should later have a change of mind and wish to be released from it? Mill acknowledges that agreements once made should not lightly be broken, and that those relating to 'money or money's worth' (i.e. commercial contracts) can reasonably be enforced by law. But his respect for individual liberty makes him reluctant to grant that, when we enter into an engagement, we bind ourselves inescapably and for ever. Not only should parties to an agreement be able to release one another from it but 'there are perhaps no contracts or engagements [other than commercial contracts] of which one can venture to say that there ought to be no liberty whatever of retractation' (V. 11).

As if to allay any uneasiness which this proposal might create, Mill points out that the law of most countries refuses to allow certain kinds of contract to stand. Contracts which violate the rights of third parties are generally outlawed, as are contracts whereby individuals sell themselves, or allow themselves to be sold, into slavery: since, as we have seen, Mill believes that 'it is not freedom to be allowed to alienate [one's] freedom'. This very significant principle, he thinks, applies across a wide range of contexts and is relevant even to the institution of marriage. Although Mill does not equate marriage with slavery, he is evidently troubled by the legal and social difficulties that society places in the way of terminating an unhappy marriage. That marriages can and do fail is, for Mill, a fact of life that needs to be addressed in a more sensitive and understanding fashion than is customary. But he is not, for once, prepared to go quite so far as his liberal precursor von Humboldt:

> Baron Wilhelm von Humboldt ... states it as his conviction, that engagements which involve personal relations or services should never be legally binding beyond a limited duration of time; and that the most important of these engagements, marriage, having the peculiarity that its objects are frustrated unless the feelings of both the parties are in harmony with it, should require nothing more than the declared will of either party to dissolve it. (V.11)

This, thinks Mill, is too quick and simple, since it takes insufficient account of the responsibilities which the parties to a marriage contract enter into.

These responsibilities are of two main kinds. First there are the duties which a husband and a wife have to fulfil the reasonable expectations that each forms of the other during the exchange of the marriage vows. By engaging to maintain their union 'for better, for worse, for richer, for poorer, in sickness and in health, till death us do part', each of the partners encourages the other to make certain commitments on the assumption that these will be reciprocated. As a result, 'a new series of moral obligations arises' on the part of each partner 'which may possibly be overruled, but cannot be ignored' (V. 11). Second, where there are children born of a marriage, the parents have responsibilities to these third parties which it has called into existence. How these are to be discharged will obviously be 'greatly affected by the continuance or disruption of the relation between the original parties to the contract'. Although Mill does not allow that 'these obligations extend to requiring the fulfilment of the contract at all costs to the happiness of the reluctant party', he insists that they are 'a necessary element in the question'.

Mill is sympathetic to von Humboldt's proposal that neither kind of responsibility should normally justify withholding the *legal* freedom of either partner to obtain a divorce from the other, but he criticizes him for underestimating the 'great difference' they make in the '*moral* freedom'. For '[a] person is bound to take all these circumstances into account before resolving on a step which may affect such important interests of others; and if he does not allow proper weight to those interests, he is morally responsible for the wrong' (V. 11). Mill's balanced and humane conclusion is that while married couples have substantial moral obligations to each other and to any children they may have, it is not the business of the law to prohibit the severance of marriage ties when their continuance would cause great unhappiness to one or both of the partners. This stance amounts to something less than the approval of divorce on demand but it is more progressive than the 1857 Divorce Act, which, though finally removing the legal right of a husband to recover possession of a runaway wife, instituted a complex, expensive and bruisingly inquisitorial procedure for applying for a divorce which left women at a considerable disadvantage to men and was well beyond the financial reach of the less affluent classes. As Geoffrey Best sums up the situation, throughout the mid-Victorian period 'the absolute rule for all sub-affluent marriages was – like it or lump it'.[14] Until long after Mill's death, divorce was to remain a luxury that only the well-off could afford.

V. 12–15: Children and their education

In these paragraphs Mill returns to a theme that has surfaced several times in *On Liberty* and whose importance he believes is often overlooked: namely, that 'liberty is often granted where it should be withheld, as well as withheld where it should be granted' (V. 12). People should be free to do as they like in their self-regarding conduct but *not* when they are exercising power over others. Here they are rightly subject to the authority of the state, which has the duty to ensure that they exercise that power with justice and discretion. But in one particularly vital area of life, that of 'family relations', the state is very neglectful in maintaining the requisite oversight and control. Husbands still retain an 'almost despotic' power over their wives, though Mill contends that this requires little treatment in the present work since the evil could be readily removed by granting to wives the same legal rights and protections that men and single women enjoy; moreover, 'the defenders of established injustice do not avail themselves of the plea of liberty, but stand forth openly as the champions of power' (V. 12). Some readers may be disappointed that Mill has no more to say about the freedom of women in a work entitled *On Liberty*, but he was unwilling to engage with so massive a subject in what was intended to be a general essay. Ten years later he rectified the omission by publishing one of the nineteenth century's most radical and powerful defences of women's rights, *The Subjection of Women*.

Mill has more to say about the issue of parents' – and especially fathers' – control over their children, precisely because the state's omission to ensure that children are properly brought up and secure from abuse is commonly justified by 'misapplied notions of liberty'. Indeed, so reluctant is the state to intervene in a father's dealings with his own children that '[o]ne would almost think that a man's children were supposed to be literally, and not metaphorically, a part of himself' (V. 12). Preventing a father from doing what he likes with his sons and daughters is considered to be an inadmissible infringement of his liberty, 'so jealous is opinion of the smallest interference of law with his absolute and exclusive control of them'. This, Mill argues, is absurd and mistaken. Consider, for instance, the case of education. To any reflective person, it must appear almost self-evident that 'the State should require and compel the education, up to a certain standard, of every human being who is born its citizen'. Yet while it is generally held to be 'one of the most sacred duties' of a parent to ensure that his child receives enough education 'to perform his part well in life towards others and towards himself', virtually no one thinks that the state should oblige him to perform it. At this point Mill, the apostle of liberty, becomes Mill the apologist for a measure of state control. Since it is just as much a parent's responsibility to provide instruction for a child's mind as food for its body, then, if he fails in this obligation, 'the State ought to see it fulfilled, at the charge, as far as possible, of the parent' (V. 12).

An obvious question that may spring to mind here is whether it would not be simpler and more effective for the government to establish a national education system rather than seek to pressure or cajole parents into seeing that their children are properly taught. (In Britain, such a system of elementary education was soon to be instituted by Forster's Education Act of 1870, which gradually swept away the motley, disorganized and very variably satisfactory assortment of educational facilities that had previously existed). To demand, as Mill does, that parents should be held responsible for their offspring's education optimistically presupposes that parents in general have the requisite judgement, financial means and opportunity to discharge this duty properly. This is a very dubious assumption in the circumstances of mid-Victorian Britain, where poverty, ignorance, squalor, crime and degradation were widespread. To many parents attempting to bring up children in an East-End 'rookery', a Manchester slum or an impoverished rural backwater, the prospect of providing their children with even the most minimally satisfactory education must have seemed about as remote as that of going to dinner with the Queen.

Mill's objection to the state's providing education as distinct from enforcing it is characteristic and predictable:

All that has been said of the importance of individuality of character, and diversity in opinions and modes of conduct, involves, as of the same unspeakable importance, diversity of education. A general State education is a mere contrivance for moulding people to be exactly like one another: ... in proportion as it is efficient and successful, it establishes a despotism over the mind, leading to one over the body (V. 13).

The objection is not so much to the *state* monopolising educational provision as to any single body doing so; Mill would be equally opposed to a national education system run by a church or any other institution likely to provide one and the same mould for all the nation's children. Only a plurality of providers can ensure that educational diversity which is an indispensable condition of the emergence of individual character. There would be nothing wrong with the state's providing an education for *some* children, so long as it did so in the spirit of 'one among many competing experiments, carried on for the purpose of example and stimulus'. Mill concedes that there is a hypothetical situation in which a society is so culturally backward that there would be no education at all unless this were supplied by the state. Only then would the state monopoly be tolerable, as the lesser of two evils; but Mill emphasizes that it would still be a very considerable evil (V. 13).

If the state is to enforce the education of children, it needs a mechanism to do it. Mill proposes a system of compulsory annual public examinations for children, which would test their level of literacy and their knowledge of facts and 'positive science'. A father whose child was found unable to read at a certain age (which Mill does not specify) 'might be subjected to a moderate fine, to be worked out, if necessary, by his labour, and the child put to school at his expense' (V. 14). Once children had obtained 'a certain minimum of general knowledge', further examinations would be voluntary and certificates could be awarded to those who had achieved set standards of proficiency. Mill responds to the obvious objection that the state might exercise 'an improper influence over opinion' via the examinations it sets by laying down that credit in examinations would always be given for knowledge of 'facts' and never for opinions. Thus '[t]he examinations on religion, politics, or other disputed topics, should not turn on the truth or falsehood of opinions, but on the matter of fact that such and such an opinion is held, on such grounds, by such authors, or schools, or churches'. And while the state must never try to bias the views of its citizens on contentious topics, 'it may very properly offer to ascertain and certify that a person possesses the knowledge requisite to make his conclusions, on any given topic, worth attending to' (V. 14).

Mill is rarely a naive writer, but it is hard to defend him against a charge of naivety in the present context. An authority which has charge of public examination arrangements effectively controls what shall be taught, and how it shall be taught, just as thoroughly as one which lays down the curriculum and trains and appoints the teachers. If the state decides, for instance, that detailed knowledge of the Bible shall be a subject of examination, then all schools will have to teach the Bible. It is also impossible to distinguish sharply 'facts' from opinions in the way that Mill would like to do. Facts are typically much more embedded in theories than his remarks indicate, and the perspectives we bring to a given subject matter have a crucial bearing on our judgements of truth and falsity. It is a commonplace in the philosophy of science that few facts, and even fewer interesting ones, are self-advertising and indisputable in the way that Mill requires. It may be a relatively plain and straightforward fact that the Norman invasion of England took place in 1066. But is it also a fact, or just an opinion, that the English were subsequently oppressed by their new rulers, or that the church in England flourished more vigorously after 1066 than before? These are matters calling for close interpretation of the evidence. And, as the Mill of chapter II is well aware, there is usually no one clearly correct view of subject matter of any significant complexity.

Any body that has exclusive control over public examinations must decide not only what the facts are in those areas of knowledge it is testing, but also which facts are important enough to be worth knowing. To be empowered to make such choices is to determine what counts as information and who shall be deemed to be well-informed. By performing the role that Mill assigns to it, the state must inevitably promote uniformity of thought and undermine the very 'diversity of education' that it is supposed to guarantee.

Mill concludes his discussion of parental obligations by defending another thesis that many would consider illiberal. Prospective parents, he holds, have no right to bring a child into the world unless they have the means to support it, and the state may legitimately prohibit people from having children where it is evident that any they have will live seriously impoverished and deprived existences (this might happen, for instance, where a country is already over-populated). Although Mill draws back from saying that the state should impose legal punishments on those who break the injunction to remain childless, he argues that they may fittingly be subjected to 'reprobation, and social stigma' (V. 15). Mill commends those states which have sought to 'forbid marriage unless the parties can show that they have the means of supporting a family', and he would presumably have supported the Chinese government's decision in the late twentieth century to impose a strict one-child-per-family rule in the face of an exponentially increasing population.

Article 12 of the modern European Convention on Human Rights lays down that 'Men and women of marriageable age have the right to marry and to found a family according to the national laws governing the exercise of this right'. This might seem to be in conflict with Mill's position and more in keeping with our contemporary ideas about the rights of individuals. Yet the Article, as John Harris has pointed out, is far from clear as it stands (does it, for instance, permit national governments under certain circumstances to take away the rights to marry and start a family, or only to regulate them?)[15] Moreover, by focusing exclusively on the rights of would-be parents it ignores another important dimension of rights, namely those of the children who might be born to them. Mill rightly observes that 'causing the existence of a human being, is one of the most responsible actions in the range of human life' (V. 15). Harris comments that Mill's 'powerful argument' 'involves the idea that one can harm people by bringing them into existence under adverse conditions' – though this also raises the question of 'how adverse the conditions must be before this becomes true'.[16] Mill's answer would probably be that people should not have children when they are unable to satisfy their basic physical needs for food, clothing and shelter, or where the only existence they can offer them is one of degradation, exploitation and ignorance – conditions antithetical to the development of valuable individual character.

It might be objected that it is one thing to say that people should exercise restraint in regard to having children when they foresee that they will find it hard to give them a tolerable upbringing, and another to hold that the state should coerce them into remaining childless. But no doubt Mill would prefer people to exercise voluntary restraint and would see state intervention only as a last resort in the case of incorrigible couples. If people do not voluntarily refrain from causing harm to others, then, by the harm principle, they may need to be restrained. Mill's views on the desirability of a policy of population control are also backed by a broader utilitarian concern with the harm that excessive population growth can do to people from the less advantaged social classes. Where too many people compete for a limited number of jobs, the inevitable effect, he notes, is to drive down wages and leave manual labourers exposed to exploitation by employers (V. 15).

Mill's contention that states need not observe an unqualified right of people to have children may seem startling coming from a writer whose views are popularly regarded as the quintessence of liberalism, yet it is entirely consistent with his exposition of the harm principle. As he himself explains, the real tension resides in the thought of his opponents:

> the current ideas of liberty, which bend so easily to real infringements of the freedom of the individual in things which concern only himself, would repel the attempt to put any restraint upon his inclinations when the consequences of their indulgence is a life or lives of wretchedness and depravity to the offspring, with manifold evils to those sufficiently within reach to be in any way affected by their actions. (V. 15)

V. 16–22: Government paternalism

Individuals should not be constrained by governments for their own good; but should governments be proactive in providing benefits for their citizens? Such state paternalism would not be objectionable on the score that it improperly restricts liberty but Mill argues that it is undesirable on other grounds. Rather than have governments provide positive benefits to their citizens, it is normally better, he suggests, for them to produce these benefits for themselves, 'individually or in voluntary combination' (V. 16).

Mill gives three reasons why this should be so. The first is that any business is generally best conducted by those who are personally interested in it. People generally know better than government what they want done, and how it may best be accomplished (V. 18). (In *The Principles of Political Economy* Mill explains that '[e]very additional function undertaken by government, is a fresh occupation imposed upon a body already overcharged with duties', as a result of which nothing is done quickly or carefully or under more than perfunctory supervision).[17] The second is that doing things for themselves rather than depending on the state is 'a mode of strengthening their active faculties, exercising their judgement, and giving them a familiar knowledge of the subjects with which they are thus left to deal' – in other words, it is a source of self-improvement, building strong and energetic character and instilling a spirit of independent self-reliance. Further, '[w]ith individuals and voluntary associations, . . . there are varied experiments, and endless diversity of experience'. The state's role should be limited to that of disseminating the results of these experiments so that others can benefit from them (V. 19). There is little point in inventing the wheel if someone else has already done it.

Mill devotes more time to the third 'and most cogent' reason for limiting the power of government, namely 'the great evil of adding unnecessarily to its power'. If 'the roads, the railways, the banks, the insurance offices, the great joint-stock companies, the universities, and the public charities', along with the organs of 'municipal corporations and local boards' were all in the hands of central government – by which Mill means under the effective control of a vast and swollen civil service – then the country would no longer be 'free otherwise than in name' (V. 20). Mill takes a dim view of state bureaucracy, seeing it as a force for conservatism and the stifling of innovation. With what might, according to taste, be viewed as prescience or prejudice, he represents the growth of modern centralized government with its comprehensive management of public affairs as inevitably productive of a dependency-culture. If the state grows greater, then individuals must grow smaller.

So strong is Mill's distaste for national bureaucracy that, unlike other left-of-centre writers of his time, he is not in favour of the introduction of competitive examinations for entrants to the British civil service. Although Queen Victoria famously complained that the use of examinations would bring into the service 'low people, without the breeding and feelings of gentlemen', the civil service reforms which began in the mid-1850s were designed to sweep away the inefficient, obstructive and self-serving government offices of the type so effectively satirized in Dickens' portrayal of the Circumlocution Office in his novel *Little Dorrit* (1855–57). Mill's own objection to examinations is not that they threaten to lower the tone of the service, but that the talented people they recruit would be better employed in other, more productive, professions. It might be thought that, if there has to be bureaucracy at all, it is better for the bureaucrats to be skilful and hard-working people rather than 'gentlemen' who expect munificent pay for a very modest input of work. But Mill is sceptical about the prospects for efficient and genuinely public-spirited service by any large bureaucracy, even one staffed by competent people. (This scepticism is perhaps ironic in view of his own thirty-five years of service as an administrator for the East India Company until its dissolution in 1858). He defends his preference for what modern political theorists call 'small government' by citing the case of Russia, where even the Tsar himself, he claims, is powerless to get things done if the 'bureaucratic body' chooses to block them – as it usually does. Where a state is run by a vast civil service, not even national revolutions are capable of effecting much real change; all that usually happens is that somebody new 'vaults into the seat' of authority, 'issues his orders to the bureaucracy, and everything goes on much as it did before; the bureaucracy being unchanged, and nobody else being capable of taking their place' (V. 20). Once a bureaucracy's power is entrenched, everyone's capacity for independent action is limited, 'the members of the bureaucracy included' (V. 21).

If Russia is an example of how *not* to do things, America is an instance of a free people who will never let themselves be 'enslaved by any man or body of men because these are able to seize and pull the reins of the central administration' (V. 21). Citizens of the United States prefer to join together and 'improvise' the means to conduct their business rather than allow distant bureaucrats to run their lives for them. Mill is not specific about the forms that such improvisation takes or about how efficiency and accountability are ensured when administrative arrangements are made on a local rather than a national basis. But he is convinced that '[n]o bureaucracy can hope to make such a people as this do or undergo anything that they do not like' (V. 21). However, his main fear appears to be not that centralised bureaucracies will make people do what they do not like, but that they will not do anything much at all. According to Mill, bureaucrats are not so much tyrants as parasites on the social body, rule-governed slaves to 'indolent routine'. This makes it even more important that state administrations do not engross all the talent in society, for able and intelligent people are needed on the outside to supply 'watchful criticism' and keep them up to the highest standards (V. 22).

V. 23: *Closing remarks on government*
Mill's criticism of 'big government', in the foregoing paragraphs, leaves him with the question of what the proper role of the state should be. In the final paragraph of *On Liberty*, Mill outlines a way to achieve 'as much of the advantages of centralised power and intelligence as can be had without turning into government channels too great a proportion of the general activity' (V. 23). The solution to the problem of governance is presented in the form of a principle: 'the greatest dissemination of power consistent with efficiency; but the greatest possible centralisation of information, and diffusion of it from the centre'. Administration should be conducted, as far as possible, at the local level, but there should be a central body to oversee the activities of local authorities and provide a repository of information for them to draw upon. This superintendent body, Mill explains, 'would concentrate, as in a focus, the variety of information and experience derived from the conduct of that branch of public business in all foreign countries, and from the general principles of political science'. It should also have the power – but no more than this – of 'compelling the local officers to obey the laws laid down for their guidance' (V. 23).

This sketch of a theory of government leaves several questions outstanding. The most pressing concern how exactly Mill conceives of the relations between the legislative, advisory and supervisory functions of the central administration. The roles he explicitly assigns to central government are a mixture of those of a library and an ombudsman; but there plainly must be more to government than this, since Mill identifies no other body to lay down the laws which local officials are expected to obey. Mill tells us that 'mischief begins' when a government, instead of calling forth the efforts of its citizens, 'substitutes its own activity for theirs; when, instead of informing, advising, and, upon occasion, denouncing, it makes them work in fetters, or bids them stand aside and does their work for them'. Yet a government which both makes and enforces the rules which local administrators must follow, controls the flow of information to those officials, oversees their operations and can 'denounce' their activities when it sees fit, in truth commands enormous power – and certainly far more than Mill, to be consistent, can think healthy. Although Mill speaks of 'the dissemination of power' down to local level, he appears not to see that the strings he attaches to the exercise of this power mean that real authority continues to rest with the central government. Local agencies may be charged with the day-to-day conduct of affairs, but they remain answerable for their acts to the central authority and must operate within its rules. In effect, they are little more than servants of the state.

In spite of its faults and unclarities, Mill's outline of a theory of government serves to remind us, at the end of *On Liberty*, of his passionate commitment to personal freedom and to forms of political organization that allow individuals to make their own experiments in living. Since 'the worth of a State, in the long run, is the worth of the individuals composing it', no political arrangements will be adequate which promote mediocrity and conformity in preference to the 'mental expansion and elevation' of the citizens. Any state, writes Mill, 'which dwarfs its men, in order that they may be more docile instruments in its hands even for beneficial purposes – will find that with small men no great thing can really be accomplished' (V. 23). To sacrifice the development of a richly various humanity for the sake of securing administrative efficiency would be to make a very poor choice indeed.

Study Questions

1. Are there any circumstances in which positive discrimination would be justified?
2. To what extent is Mill right that liberty consists in doing what one desires?

3. Should people be permitted to go nude in public if they wish?
4. Is it an affront to my liberty to prevent my selling myself into slavery?
5. May the government of an over-populated country reasonably restrict the number of children that couples are allowed to have?
6. How effective are Mill's objections to government paternalism against the modern conception of the welfare state?

PART IV

RECEPTION AND INFLUENCE

Looking back from the end of the nineteenth century, the writer and jurist Frederick Harrison reminisced about the impact of the publication of *On Liberty*:

> It is certain that the little book produced a profound impression on contemporary thought, and had an extraordinary success with the public. It has been read by hundreds of thousands, and, to some of the most vigorous and thoughtful spirits amongst us, it became a sort of gospel.[1]

The novelist Thomas Hardy in a letter of 1906 recalls that undergraduates in the 1860s knew the book 'almost by heart'.[2] Yet if *On Liberty* was eagerly devoured by readers from the moment of its appearance, it was by no means universally approved. Along with the enthusiasts who praised it to the skies for its defence of individual liberty in every sphere of life and thought were critics who judged its defence of individuality an encouragement to anarchy and indiscipline, or who saw it as a scarcely veiled attack on conventional moral values or the Protestant religion.

Many of these less sympathetic readers were worried by precisely the same issue that had troubled Mill himself, namely that people left to their own devices were far from sure to act well or wisely. 'Estimate the proportion of men and women who are selfish, sensual, frivolous, idle, absolutely commonplace and wrapped up in the smallest of petty routines,' wrote James Fitzjames Stephen, 'and consider how far the freest of free discussion is likely to improve them'. The only suitable way of dealing with such people is by 'compulsion or restraint'.[3] In *Culture and Anarchy* (1869) Matthew

Arnold grumbled that the doctrine of doing as one likes permits a person to 'march where he likes, enter where he likes, hoot as he likes, threaten as he likes, smash as he likes'.[4] While Mill would, of course, regard such bad behaviour as intolerable under the harm principle, the deeper issue that divides him from Arnold is that while Mill believes that a certain amount of imprudent or down-right foolish behaviour is a price worth paying for allowing human beings the fullest liberty in self-regarding matters, Arnold does not, seeing it as a threat to the 'right reason' and 'sweetness and light' that distinguish true culture.

But what sort of liberty is compatible with acting without wisdom or virtue, and is it a variety worth having? In a lecture delivered to the Leicester Liberal Association in 1881, T. H. Green, the White's Professor of Moral Philosophy at Oxford, warned that 'when we ... speak of freedom, we should consider carefully what we mean by it':

> We do not mean merely freedom from restraint or compulsion. We do not mean merely freedom to do as we like irrespectively of what it is that we like.... When we speak of freedom as some-thing to be so highly prized, we mean a positive power or capacity of doing or enjoying something worth doing or enjoying, and that, too, something that we do or enjoy in common with others.[5]

Compare this with Mill's thumbnail definition of liberty in Chapter V: 'liberty consists in doing what one desires' (V. 5). It is obvious at once that Green's notion of liberty is much thicker in content than Mill's (at least as Mill states it here). A person could be free in Mill's sense that no one is preventing her from doing exactly what she wants yet not be free in Green's if what she wants to do is something silly or degrading. Green agrees with Jean-Jacques Rousseau that people may have to be forced to be free. On Green's view, the 'wandering savage' has no master, but 'the freedom of savagery is not strength, but weakness', since – or so Green sup-poses, with an effortless assumption of cultural superiority – his developed powers are really less than those of 'the humblest citizen of a law-abiding state'. Only by submitting himself to 'restraint by society' will he free himself from his subjection to his own natural instincts and urges. Paradoxically, then, 'to submit is the first step in true freedom, because the first step towards the full exercise of the faculties with which man is endowed'.[6]

We need not take too seriously Green's remarks on savagery and civilization, but we should note the early appearance in his lecture of what Sir Isaiah Berlin has called a 'positive' conception of freedom, which contrasts with the predominantly 'negative' views of freedom as absence of constraint that were the norm throughout the Enlightenment period.[7] To be free in the positive sense is – roughly – to have certain capacities of deliberation and self-control and to be moved by reasonable rather than unreasonable desires; some philosophers add to this core idea that positively free individuals must also have an adequate range of practical options available to them and be able to play a part in the collective governance of their society. Some writers have understandably found the notion of positive freedom too vaguely or variously defined to be of very much use as an analytic tool, and it is sometimes claimed that the only clear conceptions of liberty are negative ones. But it is undeniable that important issues are at stake in discussions of positive liberty. We have already met, in Part III, chapter 5, Charles Taylor's view that 'the capacities relevant to freedom must involve some self-awareness, self-understanding, moral discrimination, and self-control, otherwise their exercise couldn't amount to freedom in the sense of self-direction'. Being free from external constraints (i.e. being free in the negative sense) is not such a big deal if 'we are quite self-deceived, or utterly fail to discriminate properly the ends we seek, or have lost self-control'.[8]

If positive freedom, in the core sense of rational self-mastery, is a good thing, it may nevertheless be a dangerous value to promote – or, to be more precise, there are grounds for concern that any particular attempt to 'make men free' according to a specific concept of positive freedom will be an exercise in control and manipulation. If, for instance, I believe that no one can realize his full human potential and make appropriate life-choices unless he believes in the God *I* believe in, I may do my best *in the name of his freedom* to inculcate in him the 'right' religious ideas. Although I tell myself that I am merely deciding on his behalf what his 'real' self would have chosen spontaneously had it been better informed, I am actually performing what Berlin calls a 'monstrous impersonation, which consists in equating what X would choose if he were something he is not, or at least not yet, with what X actually seeks and chooses'. This impersonation, Berlin thinks, 'is at the heart of all political theories of self-realisation'.[9] Were Green to attempt to 'civilize' his 'wandering savage' and turn him into a law-abiding citizen of Manchester or Birmingham, he would be guilty of just the impersonation that Berlin deplores.

The questions of what freedom is, and how it should (and should not) be advanced, have been at the heart of modern liberal thinking, and whilst it would be anachronistic to construe Mill as anticipating every concern of recent and contemporary writers, it is pleasant to report that *On Liberty* has continued to be regarded as a rich source of insights into some of the most challenging issues of personal freedom. One question that is often posed is to what extent Mill himself favoured a notion of positive liberty. His 'quick' definition of freedom as the ability to do as one desires without external constraint or interference is, so far as it goes, a 'negative' construal of the notion. But there is evidently a lot more to Mill's conception of freedom than that. Berlin believed that Mill (unwisely) coupled to his negative idea a much more positive one when he argued 'that men should seek to discover the truth, or ... to develop a certain type of character of which [he] approved – critical, original, ima-ginative, independent, non-conforming to the point of eccentricity, and so on'.[10]

Other readers have agreed, though without always echoing Ber-lin's disapproval of Mill's intentions. John Skorupski finds the negative and positive aspects of Mill's concept of liberty, as out-lined in the chapter 'Of individuality', organically related to each other: Mill, he says, 'defends the "negative", enlightenment concept of liberty as freedom from interference precisely in terms of the "positive", romantic concept of self-realisation'.[11] Wendy Donner likewise thinks Mill's notion of freedom anything but 'neutralist', though she emphasizes, in contrast to Berlin, that while Mill held the state responsible for ensuring that 'all citizens have the oppor-tunity to develop their generic human capacities', he also insisted 'that government not impose the *form* of development'.[12]

Of all modern writers in the liberal tradition, Joseph Raz is perhaps the one who comes closest to Mill in his defence of a conception of the good life which places individual autonomy centre-stage. A person's life is autonomous, Raz explains, 'if it is to a considerable extent his own creation'; and to be autonomous requires having 'certain mental and physical abilities and the availability of an adequate range of options' – in other words, 'positive freedom'. Hence '[p]ositive freedom is intrinsically

valuable because it is an essential ingredient and a necessary condition of the autonomous life'.[13] Like Mill, Raz believes that
autonomy is a fundamental part of our good, because the desire to
control our own life is one of our most basic desires. Yet autonomy
is not unconditionally good: thus someone whose choices are
typically selfish, trivial or downright evil is exercising autonomy but
living a life whose quality is low. Even so, Raz agrees with Mill that
others are entitled to impose constraints on him only when he
causes or threatens harm to others – which Raz proposes we think
of in terms of impeding their ability to exercise *their* autonomy and
live their lives according to their own desires.[14] Again like Mill, Raz
thinks that '[a]utonomous life is valuable only if it is spent in the
pursuit of acceptable and valuable projects and relationships'.[15]

Both Mill and Raz accept that states have a role to play in
encouraging people to employ their autonomy for good and worthy
rather than bad or trivial ends, 'so long as they do not resort to
coercion'.[16] But both support a pluralist view of values according to
which there are many alternative ways of living a good life amongst
which people may choose. (Note that the thesis of value pluralism is
not to be confused with the view that 'anything goes' and is quite
compatible with the claim that there are also some very *bad* ways of
living a human life). Where personal autonomy is treated with the
respect it merits, there should be less danger of states or other
powerful bodies seeking to mould people according to their own
ideals of what a positively free individual should be. For it should
be clear that all such attempts will be subversions of autonomy:

> It is the special character of autonomy that one cannot make
> another person autonomous. One can bring the horse to the
> water but one cannot make it drink. One is autonomous if one
> determines the course of one's life by oneself. This is not to say
> that others cannot help, but their help is by and large confined to
> securing the background conditions which enable a person to be
> autonomous.[17]

These thoughts are thoroughly Millian – which is unsurprising,
since they are inspired by Mill.

Owing less to Mill is the form of political liberalism developed by
the American political philosopher John Rawls (1921–2002). In *A
Theory of Justice* (1971), Rawls sought to establish a description of

the ideally just state by asking what ground-rules could rationally be agreed upon by a set of people who wish to form a society, but who are temporarily bereft of knowledge of their own distinguishing features, including their talents, desires and 'conception of the good', and so unable to bias the process of selection in ways which unfairly favour themselves. (Rawls describes them as making their choices behind a 'veil of ignorance', a conception which has sometimes come under fire for its artificiality but which undoubtedly serves as a powerful heuristic device). In basing his intellectual construction on the notion of a social contract, Rawls is an heir to a venerable and popular tradition in liberal theorizing, but one that was little exploited by Mill. (Rawls's theory of justice is avowedly more indebted to Immanuel Kant's idea of the legislative activities of the members of 'the kingdom of ends' – i.e. the totality of rational persons – than it is to Millian notions of individuality and autonomy). The resulting account of justice has been criticized on the ground that Rawls laid too much store by the intuitions about values and fair procedures that were common among American liberals at the date of writing, representing as being of universal validity what were really no more than the contingent preferences of a particular time and place. (For example, while Rawls is strongly committed to political egalitarianism, he shows far less sympathy with economic egalitarianism, and his dismissal of socialist values and economic theory has been seen as question-begging by some critics). Although there is no denying the power and subtlety of Rawls's articulation of the implications of his starting posits, the alternative strand of liberalism supported by writers such as Mill and Raz, though it proclaims one universal value, that of individual autonomy, is less prescriptive about just how that value shall be manifested in different social and cultural settings, since it is of its essence that people decide for themselves how to live their lives (limited only by the harm principle). One could therefore describe Mill and Raz's liberalism as being, in a sense, more liberal than Rawls's. In John Gray's words, Mill's principle of the liberty of the individual is 'a maxim for the guidance of an ideal legislator, not ... an exercise in constitution-framing'; and this feature may plausibly be thought to be to its advantage.[18]

The disagreements between Millian liberalism, on the one hand, and Rawlsian, on the other, may be thought of as a family quarrel. But how should we portray the contrast between Mill's ideas and those of another great defender of individualism from the end of the nineteenth century, the German philosopher Friedrich Nietzsche (1844–1900)? Mill died before he had a chance to read any of Nietzsche's works (the first, *The Birth of Tragedy*, appeared only a year before Mill's death), but Nietzsche read at least some of Mill's works and formed a strong dislike for both them and their author. In a well-known passage in *Beyond Good and Evil* (1886), Nietzsche scornfully dismissed Mill, along with Darwin and Herbert Spencer, as 'respectable but mediocre Englishmen' who had some capacity for recognising truths, but only those of a lowly and uninspiring kind.[19]

On the face of it, Nietzsche's contempt for Mill is surprising, since both were distressed by what they saw as the tendency of the times to encourage the pedestrian and average at the expense of the distinctive and excellent. (Mill might have been especially non-plussed to hear himself described as 'respectable' – an adjective which had for him the same negative connotations as it had for Nietzsche). 'When the masses become powerful', wrote Mill,

> an individual, or a small band of individuals, can accomplish nothing considerable except by influencing the masses; and to do this becomes daily more difficult, from the constantly increasing number of those who are vying with one another to attract the public attention. Our position, therefore, is established, that by the natural growth of civilization, power passes from individuals to masses, and the weight and importance of an individual, as compared with the mass, sink into greater and greater insignificance.[20]

Although more moderately expressed, Mill's concern here may seem not very remote from Nietzsche's:

> The *collective degeneration of man* down to that which the socialist dolts and blockheads today see as their 'man of the future' – as their ideal! – this degeneration and diminution of man to the perfect herd animal (or, as they say, to the man of the 'free society'), this animalization of man to the pygmy animal of equal rights and equal pretensions is *possible*, there is no doubt about that![21]

Whilst Mill and Nietzsche shared a common fear of the suffocating effects of modern civilization, the latter went considerably further than the former in his critique of accepted moral values. Stefan Collini has remarked how Mill, unlike Nietzsche, 'was not ... attempting fundamentally to subvert or reverse his society's moral sensibilities, but rather to refine them and call them more effectively into play on public issues'.[22] Nietzsche, by contrast, wished to take a broom to prevailing moral notions and sweep them away as so much rubbish.

Prominent amongst those that had to go were the soft and sentimental ideas of the utilitarians – 'the nonsense of the "greatest number"'.[23] In *Daybreak* (1881), Nietzsche remarks that 'In Germany it was Schopenhauer, in England John Stuart Mill who gave the widest currency to the teaching of the sympathetic affections and of pity or the advantage of others as the principle of behaviour'.[24] For Nietzsche, such teaching is mistaken because it exalts the pursuit of comfort and freedom from pain over something much more important, the painful struggle to achieve a greatness of spirit which scorns to be satisfied with the things that give pleasure to the 'herd', and which refuses to value those people (the majority of mankind) who lack similar aspirations. Those who wish to be better than this must overcome 'the petty virtues, the petty prudences, the sand-grain discretion, the ant-swarm inanity, miserable ease, the "happiness of the greatest number"'.[25] Nietzsche's main objection to Christian morality, as he construes it, is that it rewards the weak and the humble while seeking to curb the strong, energetic natures. If the meek will inherit the earth and the poor in spirit the kingdom of heaven (Matt. 5: 3, 5), then there seems little point in striving to be better than the average, since deficiencies are more profitable than qualities. Rejecting such mealy-mouthed doctrine, the Nietzschean man rises superior to the crowd and lives as a free spirit, rejoicing in the force of his own will, disposed neither to beg favours nor to do them.

Although both Mill and Nietzsche feared the levelling tendencies of the time, Mill would have viewed as preposterous Nietzsche's identification of the ideal individual with the *Übermensch* or 'overman', who has transcended ordinary human feelings and virtues and rejoices in his isolation and hatred of the 'petty people'. The claim, in *Thus Spake Zarathustra*, that 'evil is man's best strength' (since it establishes distance between the great and the also-rans and marks the ultimate rejection of stifling convention) would have struck Mill as a ludicrously perverse explication of the idea of personal excellence.[26] For Mill, great individuals transcend the mediocre and mundane, but not the brotherhood of man. Achieving Humboldt's dream of 'human development in its richest diversity' does not require the extinction of kindness and fellow-feeling, nor should these be seen as second-best virtues for those who cannot aspire to the 'higher' Nietzschean ones of hardness, pitilessness and pride in power. Millian individuals inspire the community from within rather than scoff at it from without. Nietzsche was not interested in the contributions that the great could make to society since he saw society as a collection of unworthy herd animals; time and effort spent on them was therefore wasted. Mill's much more magnanimous conception was that great individuals, via their personal achievements and excellences, enrich the texture of society, thus adding to others' value as they enhance their own.

Mill is very far from supposing, as Nietzsche alleges, that the best life for a human being is one of undemanding ease and absence of pain. As he acutely observes in *Utilitarianism*:

> A being of higher faculties requires more to make him happy, is capable probably of more acute suffering, and certainly accessible to it at more points, than one of an inferior type; but in spite of these liabilities, he can never really wish to sink into what he feels to be a lower grade of existence.[27]

'It is better', he adds, 'to be a human being dissatisfied than a pig satisfied; better to be Socrates dissatisfied than a fool dissatisfied'.[28] Mill is as aware as Nietzsche that developing oneself as an individual is never the soft option. Neither of them thinks that it would have been better for Socrates to have desisted from challenging the received wisdom of his day, though it might have prolonged his life. But Mill stresses, as Nietzsche does not, that such outstanding individuals also add something valuable to the sum of human experience on which we all can draw. Whilst Nietzsche regards the mass of human beings as incapable of substantial mental or spiritual improvement, Mill believes that individuality is the yeast that causes the general level of civilization to rise and expand, to everyone's benefit.

Mill's own highly individual and distinctive contributions to ethical and political thought are themselves a good illustration of his thesis. In the century and a half since the publication of *On Liberty* (during which the work has never been out of print), Mill's arguments have been endlessly rehearsed and re-examined, and not only in English-speaking lands. So influential has the book been in setting the parameters of discussion that it would be hard today to debate the limits of personal freedom without paying attention to the positions adopted in it. Even if one disagrees with Mill's views on the liberty of thought and expression, the 'tyranny of the majority' or the evils of paternalism, one cannot afford to ignore what he had to say about them.

And rarely, perhaps, has it been so important to pay regard to Mill's arguments than in the post-9/11 world, in which what has at times seemed an almost hysterical fear of international terrorism has driven some western governments to attempt to roll back civil liberties for the sake of the greater 'protection' of their citizens. One particularly worrying trend has been for governments to enact, or seek to enact, legislation which insists that free speech be used 'responsibly', where the determination of what counts as 'responsible' speaking is left to the state. Protest against government policies (including policies to clamp down on traditional rights not to be tortured or imprisoned without trial, or to invade or intervene in foreign countries deemed to harbour people who threaten our security), even where not formally prohibited, has increasingly been represented as irresponsible and unpatriotic – the act of a bad citizen. There are, to be sure, moral obligations attached to what we say as well as to what we do, as Mill was well aware; the harm principle forbids us to foment religious or racial hatred, or maliciously to destroy someone's reputation, or (Mill's example at III. 1) to incite a riot. It is hardly controversial that free speech may sometimes have to be subjected to a measure of restriction. But problems arise when restrictions are imposed which serve the particular objectives of governments, religions and other powerful institutions. As Philip Hensher characterizes the post-9/11 situation:

> Those who, with increasing noise, are insisting that free speech can only be permitted when it is used 'responsibly' are prescribing, across the board, a range of expression and a range of agreed opinions. That is not free speech at all. If we want to hang on to the free speech of individuals, we must personally insist on continuing the noble and long history of irresponsibility.[29]

Such 'irresponsibility' is precisely what Mill was defending in the famous remark, 'If all mankind minus one were of one opinion, and only one person were of the contrary opinion, mankind would be no more justified in silencing that one person, than he, if he had the power, would be justified in silencing mankind' (II. 1).

Governments which attempt to limit free speech on certain topics normally claim to be doing so not for any self-interested reasons but for the public good. This line, even when sincere, is unlikely to have impressed an arch-opponent of paternalism such as Mill, who thought the state had no business defending people from 'dangerous' ideas. It is in any case notoriously hard to draw boundaries with the requisite legal precision which bar only those forms of expression they are meant to.

The British Government's initial thoughts on legislation designed to outlaw the stirring up of religious hatred were a good example of what can go wrong when this difficulty is underestimated. Since religious hatreds and rivalries are a fruitful breeding-ground of violence, the attempt to constrain them by law may be justified under the harm principle. But Schedule 10 of the Serious Organised Crime and Police Bill (2004) sought to make it an offence to produce any words, behaviour, written or recorded material or public performances which, 'having regard to all the circumstances ... [are] likely to be heard or seen by any person in whom they are ... likely to stir up religious hatred'. The problem with this catch-all formulation is that some people are extremely easily aroused to feel religious hatred. On a hard-line interpretation, it could be read as forbidding *any* public oral or written criticism of any current religion, and as banning all literature (such as Shakespeare's *The Merchant of Venice*) which portrays adherents to particular religions in a negative light. (A former Lord Chancellor, the most senior law officer in England and Wales, has pointed out that under these provisions, Tony Blair could have faced prosecution for claiming in a speech in September 2001 that the atrocities in the USA were the work of religious fanatics who would have loved to have killed ten times as many people as they did).[30]

Bowing to criticism, the Government finally agreed to modify the terms of the legislation so that more weight would be placed on the *intention* to stir up religious hatred than on the hateful feelings actually generated in an audience (see the Racial and Religious Hatred Act 2006, which became law on 16 February 2006). How well or badly the new legal restrictions will serve the cause of free speech remains to be seen. Mill would not have disputed that religious hatred and intolerance are evil things but he would have disapproved of laws that make it more difficult to criticize specific religions, the truth of their doctrines or their impact on individuals and society.

The topicality of Mill's doctrines is not restricted to those concerned with freedom of thought and expression. Thus in Britain alone, recent debates on such diverse matters as the (re)classification of recreational drugs, the prohibition of smoking in public places, the right to roam at will in the countryside, the extension of pub and club licensing hours, the introduction of American-style super-casinos, and the banning of hunting with dogs have all raised issues addressed in *On Liberty*, and Mill's authority is frequently cited in support of one or another claim to freedom.

An interesting question is the extent to which Mill's 'one very simple principle' has generally been conceded by governments and public opinion. In Jonathan Riley's blunt judgement, Mill's principle of liberty 'has never gained acceptance'. At most, he thinks, 'we now have some pallid imitation, a somewhat more liberal democratic version of Judeo-Christian ethics, or American constitutionalism, which most accept more or less intuitively as providing justification for the general shape of social institutions as they have evolved'.[31] This seems to the present writer (from the other side of the Atlantic Ocean) to be too gloomy an assessment of the present status of Mill's principle. Admittedly, there are many people who do not accept the 'one very simple principle' and who would be willing to see the tentacles of state power extend much further than Mill thought tolerable. But it is equally true that there are many who do. Discussion of the various issues listed above has persistently centred on the question of whether certain kinds of behaviour cause harm to others. The argument, now accepted by Parliament, for banning smoking in pubs, shops and restaurants is that it endangers the health and reduces the comfort of other people. At the same time, powers of private landowners to restrict public access to open moorland, river banks and stretches of the sea coast have been reduced on the basis that the extension of the 'right to roam' in such areas benefits many and hurts none. There has generally been more diffidence about proposals to constrain liberty for purely paternalist ends. So while the proposal to allow 'super-casinos' has attracted some opposition from those who fear that people with a weakness for gambling will find the new temptations irresistible, this has not proved strong enough to derail the Government's plans in the absence of any convincing arguments that greater opportunities to gamble will damage third parties.

An intriguing example of the application and misapplication of Mill's views on liberty is the ongoing and bitter dispute over whether the traditional country pastime of hunting with dogs should be allowed. (Theoretically this has been illegal in England and Wales since the start of 2005, but the legislation is proving hard to enforce, partly owing to the sympathy with the hunting community felt by many policemen, judges and magistrates). Supporters of hunting vociferously complain that the banning of their 'sport' is a gross violation of their rightful liberty to amuse themselves in their own way, which they claim harms no one else. Here the main bone of contention is the *bearing* of the harm principle. Because those who wish to hunt ascribe negligible moral status to the animals (foxes, hares and, in some parts of the country, deer) they pursue, any harm caused to these counts for nothing. In contrast, opponents of hunting contend that the harm caused to the animals which the hounds tear apart is of preeminent moral significance.

Mill was decidedly of the latter way of thinking. In his essay 'Whewell on moral philosophy' he termed it a 'superstition of selfishness' to suppose that the suffering of animals was of no ethical account.[32] And he pulled no punches in a passage in the *Political Economy* which deals with cruelty to animals:

The reasons for legal intervention in favour of [mistreated] children, apply not less strongly to the case of those unfortunate slaves and victims of the most brutal part of mankind, the lower animals. It is by the grossest misunderstanding of the principles of liberty, that the infliction of exemplary punishment on ruffianism practised towards these defenceless creatures has been treated as a meddling by government with things beyond its province . . . [I]t is to be regretted that metaphysical scruples respecting the nature and source of the authority of government, should induce many warm supporters of laws against cruelty to animals, to seek for a justification of such laws in the incidental consequences of the indulgence of ferocious habits to the interests of human beings, rather than in the intrinsic merits of the case itself.[33]

Hunting and other forms of cruelty to animals may harm their practitioners by brutalizing them but the most important form of harm done is to the animal victims themselves.

Although Mill is concerned in this passage with all forms of cruelty to animals, we know his view of hunting for sport from a private letter written to John Morley in 1869. Referring to an anti-field-sports article published by the historian Edward Augustus Freeman, Mill says:

> I cannot too much congratulate you on such a paper as that of Mr Freeman. I honour him for having broken ground against field sports, a thing I have often been tempted to do myself, but having so many unpopular causes already on my hands, thought it wiser not to provoke fresh hostility.[34]

Those who hunt for amusement cannot use the utilitarian argument that they need to kill animals as a means of survival, as some aboriginal hunters of wild animals can. Killing or mistreating animals for sport, on Mill's view, is unambiguously ruled out by the harm principle, just as killing or mistreating human beings for the sadistic pleasure it gives one would be. Therefore claims that it is a legitimate liberty of Englishmen are quite specious.

In a recent reappraisal of Mill, John Skorupski fittingly describes his philosophy as 'one of the main land masses in the ocean' of nineteenth-century thought, alongside those of Marx, Hegel and Nietzsche.[35] As we know, intellectual land masses share with their physical counterparts a tendency to rise and fall. The forces of criticism mould, cut away at, create faults and fissures in, but can also add height and substance to existing eminences of thought. At present, the peaks of Marx and Hegel appear less lofty than they did a few decades ago, while that of Nietzsche is rising sharply. Respect for the quality of Mill's philosophy has also grown over the last half century, as the difficulties of defining a form of liberalism suitable for our times have caused thinkers on the left of centre to look more and more to Mill for guidance. Mill and Humboldt's emphasis on the 'absolute and essential importance of human development in its richest diversity' remains vitally relevant today, when individuality is as much in danger as it ever was from opinionated governments and religious and other forces for ideological conformity.

If individualism is a paramount theme in both Mill and Nietzsche, Mill takes more seriously the fact that man is a social animal, and that our aspirations for self-development will be defeated if the communities we live in are fractured by mutual hostility, intolerance and selfishness. On the face of it, insisting on the value of individuality and 'doing one's own thing' might be thought an encouragement to a self-indulgent neglect of the interests of other people. (A related worry, expressed by Martha Nussbaum, is that by reserving special praise for those who develop their genius, Mill is implicitly less respectful than he should be towards people of more ordinary abilities and attainments).[36] But Mill believes that the development of individual excellences of mind and character benefits both their subjects *and* their communities, and that honour is due to all who exercise their autonomy in making the most of their natural potential, be the outcome great or modest. For Mill's form of utilitarianism, which regards the interests of 'man as a progressive being', individual and social good finally dovetail, since the mental and moral qualities which add value to individuals' lives enrich their societies too.

Writing in 1883, Mill's biographer Alexander Bain said of him that 'No calculus can integrate the innumerable little pulses of knowledge and of thought that he has made to vibrate in the minds of his generation'.[37] In 2006, the bicentenary of Mill's birth, we can add: and in the minds of many subsequent generations too. No work of his, as he himself predicted, has resonated with the reading public so much as *On Liberty*, which has continued to impress by its incisive argumentation, its intense concern for individual and public good, and its invigorating combination of optimism about human possibilities with warning of the threats they face under the conditions of modern life. In the final analysis, *On Liberty* is not merely a theoretical disquisition on freedom but a practical manual on how to be free: a book to be lived as well as read.

Bain reports how Charles Kingsley thanked Mill for a copy of the work, claiming that it had 'affected me by making me a clearer-headed, braver-minded man on the spot'.[38] Kingsley was flattering Mill, but only a little. *On Liberty* is one of those rare philosophical texts that genuinely merit the epithet 'inspiring'. A century and a half after its first appearance, it still has the capacity to startle, to excite and to move. We may hope that a hundred and fifty years from now it will still be doing the same, helping to protect the values of free thought and individuality against the ever-present pressures towards conformity and mediocrity that thrive under the unwinking eye of Big Brother.

GUIDE TO READING

A. WORKS BY MILL

1. General
The standard modern edition is the *Collected Works of John Stuart Mill*, general editor J.M. Robson (Toronto and London: University of Toronto Press and Routledge & Kegan Paul), 33 volumes, 1963–91. Works by Mill referred to in this Reader's Guide are located in this edition as follows:

> *Autobiography*, in *Autobiography and Literary Essays*, vol.1, pp.1–290.
> 'Civilization', in *Essays on Politics and Society*, vol.18, pp.117–48.
> 'Coleridge', in *Essays on Ethics, Religion, and Society*, vol.10, pp.117–64.
> *Considerations on Representative Government*, in *Essays on Politics and Society*, vol.19, pp.371–578.
> 'De Tocqueville on democracy in America' (I and II), in *Essays on Politics and Society*, vol.18, pp.47–90, 153–204.
> *Earlier Letters, 1812–1848*, vols.12, 13.
> 'Grote's History of Greece [II]', in *Essays on Philosophy and the Classics*, vol.11, pp.307–38.
> *Later Letters, 1849–1873*, vols.14–17.
> *On Liberty*, in *Essays on Politics and Society*, vol.18, pp.213–310.
> *Principles of Political Economy*, vols.2, 3.
> *Public and Parliamentary Speeches*, vols.28, 29.
> *The Subjection of Women*, in *Essays on Equality, Law, and Education*, vol.21, pp.259–340.
> *Utilitarianism*, in *Essays on Ethics, Religion, and Society*, vol.10, pp.203–60.
> 'Whewell on moral philosophy', in *Essays on Ethics, Religion, and Society*, vol.10, pp.165–202.

2. Editions of On Liberty
On Liberty has been reprinted many times and there is a large number of good-quality inexpensive editions. The following is a small selection of these.

On Liberty, ed. Alexander, Edward (Peterborough, Ontario: Broadview Press, 1999).

On Liberty and Other Writings, ed. Collini, Stefan (Cambridge: Cambridge University Press, 1989).

On Liberty, ed. Gray, John (Oxford: Oxford University Press, 1998).

On Liberty, ed. Himmelfarb, Gertrude (Harmondsworth: Penguin, 1982).

On Liberty, in *Utilitarianism, Liberty and Representative Government*, ed. Lindsay, A.D. (London: Everyman's Library, 1910).

On Liberty, in *Utilitarianism, Liberty and Representative Government*, ed. Williams, Geraint (London: Everyman's Library, 1993).

On Liberty, in *On Liberty and the Subjection of Women*, ed. O'Grady, Jane (Ware: Wordsworth Classics, 1996).

On Liberty, ed. Rapaport, Elizabeth (Indianapolis, IL: Hackett Publishing Company, 1978).

On Liberty (New York: Dover Publications, 2002).

B. WORKS BY OTHER AUTHORS

The secondary literature relevant to *On Liberty* is enormous. The list that follows includes all works referred to in this Reader's Guide, plus a small selection of further useful titles.

Ali, Monica, 'Do we need laws on hatred?' in Appignanesi, Lisa (ed.), *Free Expression*, pp.47–58.

Appiah, Kwame Anthony, *The Ethics of Identity* (Princeton and Oxford: Princeton University Press, 2005).

Appignanesi, Lisa (ed.), *Free Expression is No Offence* (London: Penguin, 2005).

Arneson, Richard J., 'Mill versus paternalism', *Ethics*, 90, 1980, pp.470–89.

Arnold, Matthew, *Culture and Anarchy* (Cambridge: Cambridge University Press, 1957).

Bain, Alexander, *John Stuart Mill. A Criticism with Personal Recollections* (London: Longmans, Green, and Company, 1882).

Benn, S.I., *A Theory of Freedom* (Cambridge: Cambridge University Press, 1988).

Bentham, Jeremy, 'Anarchical fallacies', *The Works of Jeremy Bentham*, vol.2 (Edinburgh: Tait, 1843).

Berger, Fred, *Happiness, Justice, and Freedom: the Moral and Political Philosophy of John Stuart Mill* (Berkeley, CA: University of California Press, 1984).

Berlin, Isaiah, *Four Essays on Liberty* (London: Oxford University Press, 1969) [contains the essays 'Two concepts of liberty', pp.118–72, and 'John Stuart Mill and the ends of life', pp.173–206].

Best, Geoffrey, *Mid-Victorian Britain 1851–75* (London: Fontana, 1979).

Blanshard, Brand, *On Philosophical Style* (Manchester: Manchester University Press, 1954).

Braybrooke, David, *Utilitarianism: Restorations, Repairs, Renovations* (Toronto: University of Toronto Press, 2004).

Brown, D.G., 'Mill on liberty and morality', *The Philosophical Review*, 81, 1972, pp.133–58.

Collini, Stefan, *Public Moralists: Political Thought and Intellectual Life in Britain, 1850–1930* (Oxford: Clarendon Press, 1991).

Constant, Benjamin *The Spirit of Conquest and Usurpation and Their Relation to European Civilization*, in *Political Writings*, ed. Fontana, Biancamaria (Cambridge: Cambridge University Press, 1988).

Cowling, Maurice, *Mill and Liberalism* (Cambridge: Cambridge University Press, 1963; second, rev. ed, 1990).

Devlin, Patrick, *The Enforcement of Morals* (London: Oxford University Press, 1965).

Dickens, Charles, *Little Dorrit* (many editions; orig. pub. 1855–57).

Donner, Wendy, *The Liberal Self: John Stuart Mill's Moral and Political Philosophy* (Ithaca and London: Cornell University Press, 1991).

Dworkin, Ronald, *Taking Rights Seriously* (London: Duckworth, 1977).

Eisenach, Eldon J. (ed.), *Mill and the Moral Character of Liberalism* (University Park, PA: Pennsylvania State University Press, 1998).

Epstein, Jason, 'Mystery in the heartland', *New York Review of Books*, 51, 7 October 2004, pp.8–9.

Feinberg, Joel, 'The child's right to an open future', in Howie, J. (ed.), *Ethical Principles for Social Policy* (Carbondale, IL: Southern Illinois University Press, 1983), pp.97–122.

—— *Freedom and Fulfillment* (Princeton: Princeton University Press, 1993).

—— *The Moral Limits of the Criminal Law*, four vols., (New York: Oxford University Press, 1984–1988).

—— *Rights, Justice, and the Bounds of Liberty* (Princeton: Princeton University Press, 1980).

Geuss, Raymond, *Public Goods, Private Goods* (Princeton and Oxford: Princeton University Press, 2003).

Gray, John, *Berlin* (London: Fontana, 1995).

—— *Mill on Liberty: A Defence*, 2nd ed. (London and New York: Routledge, 1996).

Gray, John and Smith, G.W. (eds.), *J.S. Mill: On Liberty in Focus* (London: Routledge, 1991).

Green T.H., 'Liberal legislation and freedom of contract', in Miller, David (ed.), *The Liberty Reader*, pp.21–32.

Habib, Don A., *John Stuart Mill and the Ethic of Human Growth* (Dordrecht: Kluwer, 2001).

Hamburger, Joseph, *John Stuart Mill on Liberty and Control* (Princeton and Oxford: Princeton University Press, 2001).

Harris, John, 'The right to found a family', in Scarre, Geoffrey (ed.), *Children, Parents and Politics* (Cambridge: Cambridge University Press, 1989), pp.133–53.

Hart, H.L.A., *Law, Liberty and Morality* (London: Oxford University Press, 1963).

Hayek, F.A., *John Stuart Mill and Harriet Taylor: Their Correspondence and Subsequent Marriage* (London: Routledge and Kegan Paul, 1951).

Hensher, Philip, 'Free speech responsibly', in Appignanesi, Lisa (ed.), *Free Expression*, pp.73–77.

Himmelfarb, Gertrude, *On Liberty and Liberalism: The Case of John Stuart Mill* (New York: Knopf, 1974).

Hoag, Robert W., 'Happiness and freedom: recent work on John Stuart Mill', *Philosophy and Public Affairs*, 15, 1986, pp.188–99.

Honderich, Ted, '*On Liberty* and morality-dependent harms', *Political Studies*, 30, 1982, pp.504–14.

Humboldt, Wilhelm von, *The Sphere and Duties of Government*, tr. Coulthard, Joseph (London: Chapman, 1854; facsimile reprint, Bristol: Thoemmes Press, 1996).

Illustrated London News, The, 35, 1859.

Ishiguro, Kazuo, *The Remains of the Day* (New York: Knopf, 1989).

Johnson, Lyndon B., 'Commencement address at Howard University, 4 June 1965', http://www.lbjlib.utexas/johnson.archives.hom.speeches.hom/650604.asp.

Kinzer, B.L., Robson, A.P., and Robson, J.M., *A Moralist in and out of Parliament: J.S. Mill at Westminster, 1865–68* (Toronto: University of Toronto Press, 1992).

Kramer, M., *The Quality of Freedom* (Oxford: Oxford University Press, 2003).

Kurer, Oskar, *John Stuart Mill: the Politics of Progress* (New York and London: Garland Publishing, Inc., 1991).

Levin, Michael, *J.S. Mill on Civilization and Barbarism* (London and New York: Routledge, 2004).

Locke, John, 'A letter concerning toleration', in *The Second Treatise of Civil Government and A Letter Concerning Toleration*, ed. Gough, J.W. (Oxford: Blackwell, 1946).

—— *An Essay Concerning Human Understanding*, ed. Yolton, John, two vols. (London: Everyman's Library, rev. ed., 1965).

Lyons, David, 'Mill's theory of morality', *Nous*, 10, 1976, pp.101–20.

—— *Rights, Welfare, and Mill's Moral Theory* (New York and Oxford: Oxford University Press, 1994).

Mendus, Susan, *Toleration and the Limits of Liberalism* (London: Macmillan, 1989).

Miller, David (ed.), *The Liberty Reader* (Edinburgh: Edinburgh University Press, 2006).

Milton, John, *Areopagitica* (facsimile reprint of the 1st ed., 1644, Menston: Scolar Press, 1968).

Mueller, Iris Wessel, *John Stuart Mill and French Thought* (Urbana, IL: University of Illinois Press, 1956).

Myerson, George, *Mill's On Liberty: A Beginner's Guide* (London: Hodder and Stoughton, 2001).

Nicholls, James Quan, 'Alcohol in liberal thought', *International Journal of Cultural Studies*, 9, 2006, pp.131–51.

Nietzsche, Friedrich, *Beyond Good and Evil*, tr. Hollingdale, R.J. (London: Penguin, rev. ed., 1990).
—— *A Nietzsche Reader*, tr. and ed. Hollingdale, R.J. (London: Penguin, 1977).
—— *The Will to Power*, tr. Kaufmann, Walter and Hollingdale,R.J. (New York: Vintage Books, 1968).
—— *Thus Spake Zarathustra*, tr. Hollingdale, R.J. (Harmondsworth: Penguin, 1961).
Nussbaum, Martha, *Hiding from Humanity: Disgust, Shame, and the Law* (Princeton and Oxford: Princeton University Press, 2004.
Owen, David Edward, *English Philanthropy, 1660–1960* (Cambridge, MA: Belknap Press, 1965).
Pettit, Philip, *A Theory of Freedom* (Cambridge: Polity Press, 2001).
Plamenatz, John, *The English Utilitarians*, 2nd ed. (Oxford: Blackwell, 1965).
Pyle, Andrew (ed.), *Liberty: Contemporary Responses to John Stuart Mill* (Bristol: Thoemmes Press, 1994).
Rawls, John, *A Theory of Justice* (Cambridge, MA: Harvard University Press, 1971).
Raz, Joseph, *The Morality of Freedom* (Oxford: Clarendon Press, 1986).
Rees, John, *John Stuart Mill's On Liberty* (Oxford: Clarendon Press, 1985).
Riley, Jonathan, ' "One very simple principle" ', *Utilitas*, 3, 1991, pp.217–44.
—— *Routledge Philosophy Guidebook to Mill on Liberty* (London and New York: Routledge, 1998).
Ryan, Alan, *J.S. Mill* (London: Routledge and Kegan Paul, 1974).
—— 'Mill in a liberal landscape', in Skorupski, John (ed.), *The Cambridge Companion to Mill*, pp.497–540.
Scarre, Geoffrey, 'Children and paternalism', *Philosophy*, 55, 1980, pp.117–24.
Singer, Peter, ed., *Applied Ethics* (Oxford: Oxford University Press, 1986).
Skorupski, John (ed.), *The Cambridge Companion to John Stuart Mill* (Cambridge: Cambridge University Press, 1998).
—— *John Stuart Mill* (London and New York: Routledge, 1989).
—— *Why Read Mill Today?* (London and New York: Routledge, 2006).
Stafford, William, *John Stuart Mill* (Basingstoke: Macmillan, 1998)
Stephen, James Fitzjames, *Liberty, Equality, Fraternity* (Indianapolis: Liberty Fund, 1993; original edition 1873).
Taylor, Charles, 'What's wrong with negative liberty?' in Miller, David (ed.), *The Liberty Reader*, pp.141–62.
Ten, C.L., *Mill on Liberty* (Oxford: Clarendon Press, 1980).
—— (ed.), *Mill's Moral, Political and Legal Philosophy* (Aldershot: Ashgate and Dartmouth Publishing Co., 1999).
Thomas, William, *Mill* (Oxford: Oxford University Press, 1985).
Tocqueville, Alexis de, *Democracy in America*, tr. Bowen, Francis (rev.

Bradley, Phillips), two vols. in one (London: Everyman's Library, 1994).

Turk, Christopher, *Coleridge and Mill: a Study of Influence* (Aldershot: Ashgate, 1988).

Vernon, R., 'John Stuart Mill and pornography: beyond the harm principle', *Ethics*, 106, 1996, pp.621–32.

West, Henry (ed.), *The Blackwell Guide to Mill's Utilitarianism* (Oxford: Blackwell, 2006).

Williams, Bernard, *In the Beginning was the Deed: Realism and Moralism in Political Argument* (Princeton and Oxford: Princeton University Press, 2005).

Wilson, A.N., *The Victorians* (London: Arrow Books, 2003).

Wolff, Jonathan, 'Mill, indecency and the liberty principle', *Utilitas*, 10, 1998, pp.1–16.

Young, R., *Personal Autonomy: Beyond Negative and Positive Liberty* (London and Sydney: Croom Helm, 1986).

NOTES

PART I

1. John Stuart Mill, *Utilitarianism*, ch.2, para.2.
2. Mill, *Utilitarianism*, ch.2, para.4.
3. Brand Blanshard, *On Philosophical Style*, p.24.
4. John Stuart Mill, *Autobiography, Collected Works*, vol.1, p.249; Gertrude Himmelfarb, *On Liberty and Liberalism*, p.249.
5. Mill, *Utilitarianism*, ch.2, para.5.
6. Mill, 'Genius', *Collected Works*, vol.1, p.330.
7. Mill, *Earlier Letters, 1812–1848, Collected Works*, vol.12, p.84.
8. John Rees, *John Stuart Mill's On Liberty*, p.71.
9. Maurice Cowling, *Mill and Liberalism*, p.104.
10. William Stafford, *John Stuart Mill*, p.99.
11. Mill, *Autobiography, Collected Works*, vol.1, p.261.
12. Mill, *Autobiography, Collected Works*, vol.1, pp.257/59.
13. Mill, *Autobiography, Collected Works*, vol.1, p.195.
14. Alexander Bain, *John Stuart Mill*, p.168.
15. Bain, *John Stuart Mill*, p.171.
16. Himmelfarb, *On Liberty and Liberalism*, p.225.
17. Himmelfarb, *On Liberty and Liberalism*, pp.225–26.
18. Mill, *Autobiography, Collected Works*, vol.1, p.259.
19. Mill, *Autobiography, Collected Works*, vol.1, p.259.

PART III. CHAPTER I

1. John Stuart Mill, 'De Tocqueville on Democracy in America [II]', *Collected Works*, vol.18, p.194.
2. Mill, 'De Tocqueville on Democracy in America [II]', *Collected Works,* vol.18, p.190.
3. A. de Tocqueville, *Democracy in America*, vol.1, pp.259, 261.
4. De Tocqueville, *Democracy in America*, vol.1, pp.263, 264.
5. Alan Ryan, 'Mill in a liberal landscape', p.500.
6. Benjamin Constant, *The Spirit of Conquest*, p.102.

7. Constant, *The Spirit of Conquest*, p.103.
8. Constant, *The Spirit of Conquest*, p.104.
9. Andrew Pyle (ed.), *Liberty: Contemporary Responses to John Stuart Mill*, p.82.
10. Pyle (ed.), *Liberty: Contemporary Responses*, p.218.
11. Mill, *Autobiography, Collected Works*, vol.1, p.259.
12. Mill, *Autobiography, Collected Works*, vol.1, pp.259/61.
13. John Locke, 'A letter concerning toleration', p.128.
14. *The Illustrated London News*, 12 November 1859, p.464.
15. Joel Feinberg, 'The child's right to an open future', p.98.
16. James Fitzjames Stephen, *Liberty, Equality, Fraternity*, pp.19–20.
17. Mill, *Autobiography, Collected* Works, vol.1, p.260.
18. Locke, 'A letter concerning toleration', pp.151–52.
19. Mill, *Autobiography, Collected Works*, vol.1, p.259.
20. Joseph Raz, *The Morality of Freedom*, p.420; my emphasis.
21. Jeremy Bentham, 'Anarchical fallacies', p.501.
22. John Gray, *Berlin*, p.8.
23. Thomas Carlyle, quoted in *On Liberty*, ed. Alexander, Edward, Appendix C: Comments by Contemporaries about *On Liberty* and Mill, p.184.

PART III. CHAPTER II

1. John Gray, *Mill on Liberty: A Defence*, p.110.
2. C.L. Ten, *Mill on Liberty*, p.136.
3. Gray, *Mill on Liberty*, p.106; see on the same topic John Skorupski, *Why Read Mill Today?* pp.56–61.
4. Cited in Ten, *Mill on Liberty*, p.133.
5. Bain, *John Stuart Mill*, p.104
6. Quoted in Jason Epstein, 'Mystery in the heartland', p.9.
7. John Skorupski, *John Stuart Mill*, p.380.
8. Patrick Devlin, *The Enforcement of Morals*, p.114.
9. Devlin, *The Enforcement of Morals*, p.13; my emphasis.
10. Devlin, *The Enforcement of Morals*, p.25.
11. Devlin, *The Enforcement of Morals*, p.111.
12. John Milton, *Areopagitica*, p.26.
13. Bain, *John Stuart Mill*, pp.104–05.
14. Stephen, *Liberty, Equality, Fraternity*, p.36.
15. Mill, 'Civilization', *Collected Works*, vol.18, p.134.
16. Mill, 'Civilization', *Collected Works*, vol.18, p.138.
17. Mill, 'Coleridge', *Collected Works*, vol.10, pp.146–48.
18. For a fuller analysis of Victorian religious practice, see Geoffrey Best, *Mid-Victorian Britain, 1851–75*, ch.3.
19. Mill, *Utilitarianism*, ch.2, para.4.
20. Mill, *Utilitarianism*, ch.2, para.6.
21. Bain, *John Stuart Mill*, p.105.
22. Bain, *John Stuart Mill*, p.106.

23. Pyle, *Liberty: Contemporary Responses*, p.251.
24. Pyle, *Liberty: Contemporary Responses*, p.252.

PART III. CHAPTER III

1. Mill, *Autobiography, Collected Works*, vol.1, p.259.
2. Mill, *Autobiography, Collected Works*, vol.1, p.260.
3. Wilhelm von Humboldt, *The Sphere and Duties of Government*, p.11.
4. Mill, 'Civilization', *Collected Works*, vol.18, p.129.
5. Mill, 'Civilization', *Collected Works*, vol.18, p.126.
6. Wendy Donner, *The Liberal Self: John Stuart Mill's Moral and Political Philosophy*, p.150.
7. Mill, *Utilitarianism*, ch.2, para.4.
8. For more on the resemblances and differences between Mill and Nietzsche, see below, Part IV.
9. John Stuart Mill, 'Grote's History of Greece [II]', *Collected Works*, vol.14, pp.333–34.
10. John Stuart Mill, *Considerations on Representative Government, Collected Works*, vol.19, p.396.
11. Pyle, *Contemporary Responses*, p.218.
12. Pyle, *Contemporary Responses*, p.229.
13. Pyle, *Contemporary Responses*, p.209.
14. Isaiah Berlin, *Four Essays on Liberty*, p.178.
15. Kwame Anthony Appiah, *The Ethics of Identity*, p.11.
16. Appiah, *The Ethics of Identity*, p.10.
17. Gray, *Mill on Liberty*, p.142.
18. Berlin, *Four Essays*, p.194.
19. Best, *Mid-Victorian Britain, 1851–75*, p.256.
20. Best, *Mid-Victorian Britain, 1851–75*, p.255.
21. Stephen, *Liberty, Equality, Fraternity*, p.31.
22. Stephen, *Liberty, Equality, Fraternity*, p.32.
23. Stephen, *Liberty, Equality, Fraternity*, p.33.
24. Stephen, *Liberty, Equality, Fraternity*, p.34.
25. Stephen, *Liberty, Equality, Fraternity*, p.34n.
26. Stephen, *Liberty, Equality, Fraternity*, p.34n.

PART III. CHAPTER IV

1. Bain, *John Stuart Mill*, pp.107–08.
2. Locke, 'A letter concerning toleration', pp.151–52.
3. Bain, *John Stuart Mill*, p.109.
4. The speech is conveniently reprinted in Peter Singer (ed.), *Applied Ethics*, pp.97–104.
5. Himmelfarb, *On Liberty and Liberalism*, p.100.
6. Bain, *John Stuart Mill*, p.70.
7. John Stuart Mill, 'Whewell on moral philosophy', *Collected Works*, vol.10, p.178.

8. Mill, 'Whewell on moral philosophy', *Collected Works*, vol.10, p.177.
9. Mill, 'Whewell on moral philosophy', *Collected Works*, vol.10, p.179.
10. Gray, *Mill on Liberty*, p.95.
11. Skorupski, *John Stuart Mill*, p.360.
12. Himmelfarb, *On Liberty and Liberalism*, p.96.
13. Ten, *Mill on Liberty*, p.92.
14. Mill, 'Coleridge', *Collected Works*, vol.10, pp.133–34.
15. Ten, *Mill on Liberty*, p.95.
16. Mill, 'Coleridge', *Collected Works*, vol.10, p.134.
17. Riley, *Routledge Philosophy Guidebook to Mill on Liberty*, p.170.
18. Riley, *Routledge Philosophy Guidebook to Mill on Liberty*, p.168.
19. Raymond Geuss, *Public Goods, Private Goods*, p.86.
20. Mill, 'Coleridge', *Collected Works*, vol.10, p.134.

PART III. CHAPTER V

1. Mill, *Principles of Political Economy, Collected Works*, vol.3, p.938.
2. For the full text of Johnson's speech, see http://www.lbjlib.utexas.edu/johnson/archives.hom/speeches.hom/650604.asp.
3. John Locke, *An Essay Concerning Human Understanding*, Bk.II.ch.x-xi.para.56; vol.1, p.223.
4. Bernard Williams, *In the Beginning was the Deed: Realism and Moralism in Political Argument*, p.79.
5. Charles Taylor, 'What's wrong with negative liberty?' p.146.
6. See Michael Levin, *J.S. Mill on Civilization and Barbarism*, pp.101–04, for a fuller discussion of Mill's sympathy with Palmerston's gunboat diplomacy.
7. Ronald Dworkin, *Taking Rights Seriously*, p.236.
8. Joel Feinberg, *Rights, Justice, and the Bounds of Liberty*, p.89.
9. Ten, *Mill on Liberty*, p.102.
10. Feinberg, *Rights, Justice, and the Bounds of Liberty*, p.89.
11. Jonathan Wolff, 'Mill, indecency and the liberty principle', p.8.
12. Wolff, 'Mill, indecency and the liberty principle', p.10
13. Wolff, 'Mill, indecency and the liberty principle', p.11.
14. Best, *Mid-Victorian Britain, 1851–75*, p.304.
15. John Harris, 'The right to found a family', p.134.
16. Harris, 'The right to found a family', p.140.
17. Mill, *Principles of Political Economy, Collected Works*, vol.3, p.940.

PART IV

1. See Himmelfarb, *On Liberty and Liberalism*, p.295.
2. Quoted in Himmelfarb, *On Liberty and Liberalism*, p.296.
3. Stephen, *Liberty, Equality, Fraternity*, p.23.
4. Matthew Arnold, *Culture and Anarchy*, p.76.
5. T.H. Green, 'Liberal legislation and freedom of contract', p.21.
6. Green, 'Liberal legislation and freedom of contract', p.22.

7. See Berlin, 'Two concepts of liberty', *passim*, in *Four Essays on Liberty*.
8. Taylor, 'What's wrong with negative liberty?' p.146.
9. Berlin, *Four Essays on Liberty*, pp.133–34.
10. Berlin, *Four Essays on Liberty*, p.128.
11. Skorupski, *John Stuart Mill*, p.343.
12. Donner, *The Liberal Self*, pp.126, 127.
13. Raz, *The Morality of Freedom*, pp.408–09.
14. Raz, *The Morality of Freedom*, pp.412–15.
15. Raz, *The Morality of Freedom*, p.417.
16. Raz, *The Morality of Freedom*, p.420.
17. Raz, *The Morality of Freedom*, p.407.
18. Gray, *Mill on Liberty*, p.148.
19. Friedrich Nietzsche, *Beyond Good and Evil*, section 253, pp.184–85.
20. Mill, 'Civilization', *Collected Works*, vol.18, p.126.
21. Nietzsche, *Beyond Good and Evil*, section 203, pp.127–28.
22. Stefan Collini, *Public Moralists: Political Thought and Intellectual Life in Britain, 1850–1930*, p.130.
23. Nietzsche, *Beyond Good and Evil*, section 203, p.126.
24. Friedrich Nietzsche, *A Nietzsche Reader*, p.94.
25. Friedrich Nietzsche, *Thus Spake Zarathustra*, 'Of the higher man', section 3, p.298.
26. Nietzsche, 'Of the higher man', section 5, p.299.
27. Mill, *Utilitarianism*, ch.2, para.6.
28. Mill, *Utilitarianism*, ch.2, para.6.
29. Philip Hensher, 'Free speech responsibly', p.77.
30. Cited by Monica Ali, 'Do we need laws on hatred?' p.53.
31. Riley, *Routledge Philosophy Guidebook to Mill on Liberty*, p.33.
32. Mill, 'Whewell on moral philosophy', *Collected Works*, vol.10, p.186.
33. Mill, *Principles of Political Economy, Collected Works*, vol.3, p.952.
34. Mill, *Later Letters, 1849–73, Collected Works*, vol.17, pp.1673–74.
35. Skorupski, 'Why read Mill today?' p.xi.
36. Martha Nussbaum, *Hiding from Humanity: Shame, Disgust, and the Law*, p.331.
37. Bain, *John Stuart Mill*, p.195.
38. Bain, *John Stuart Mill*, p.38.

INDEX